25 WAYS TO

Show Love

TO YOUR WIFE

25 WAYS TO
Show Love
TO YOUR WIFE

Doug Flanders, M.D.

Prescott Publishing

TYLER, TEXAS

25 Ways to Show Love to Your Wife.
Copyright ©2014 by Doug Flanders.

Cover design, interior design, and typesetting:
Jennifer Flanders

Cover photos:
Microsoft Office Stock Photos (front)
Jennifer Flanders (back)

ISBN: 978-1-938945-09-0
LCCN: 2015932308

FIRST EDITION
10 9 8 7 6 5 4 3 2 1

To my lovely wife, Jennifer.
Thanks for making it so easy to love you.

- Contents -

Where's the Love?

Introduction

Love God. Love others.

When Jesus was asked to name the most important commandment, this was His reply in a nutshell. He answered plainly:

> *"You shall love the Lord your God with all your heart and with all your soul and with all your mind. This is the first and greatest commandment. And the second is like it: Love your neighbor as yourself. All the Law and the Prophets hang on these two commandments."* (Matthew 22:37-40, NIV)

Even the Ten Commandments are an expanded version of this idea. Every law ever written essentially defines layer upon layer of detail built on this same simple concept.

But despite this clear, straightforward reply, Christ's listeners immediately start making excuses: *"And who is my neighbor?"* they ask, hoping to justify themselves.[1]

Already they're looking for loopholes.

Sometimes as Christians, what we lack is not *knowledge*, but *willpower*.

> "Love is life.
> And if you
> miss love,
> you miss life."
>
> - Leo Buscaglia

We know that loving God and loving others is what we are supposed to be doing, but living by that principle is often difficult. It pulls us out of our comfort zone. It requires sacrifice.

And sacrifice is never easy.

Our relationship with God and with our fellow man is ultimately a heart issue. If our heart is intent on love, we will find ways to love. If not, we'll find every excuse not to.

If our hearts are right, simple rules are enough.

If our hearts are wrong, no amount of detail can close the loopholes.

For husbands, loving one's neighbor will obviously include loving your wife. In that she shares your house, your table, your room, and your bed, your wife is the closest neighbor you will ever have.

But Scripture doesn't stop here. It raises the bar even higher by clearly spelling out a husband's responsibility:

"Husbands, love your wives, just as Christ also loved the church and gave Himself up for her." (Ephesians 5:25, NASB)

So now I am to love my wife in the same way that Christ loves me. That takes things to a whole new level, doesn't it? It is of vital importance that we, as husbands, rise to meet this challenge. The health and success of our marriages, our families, our churches, and our communities depend upon how well we do our job.

> "A loving heart is the truest wisdom."
>
> - Charles Dickens

Not only is our love a Biblical imperative, but it is also the distinguishing mark of a Christian. Jesus said, *"By this all men will know that you are My disciples, if you have love for one another."* (John 13:35, NASB)

To which John adds, *"If someone says, 'I love God,' and hates his brother, he is a liar; for the one who does not love his brother whom he has seen, cannot love God whom he has not seen."* (1 John 4:20, NASB)

Surely the same truth applies to any husband who claims to love God, but doesn't love his wife. Yet, when nearly half of all marriages end in divorce, even within the church, this is where many of us are living today.

Marriage is in trouble.

It is in trouble because we have failed in our duty to love. We've bought into the world's idea that love is a feeling—powerful and intense, to be sure, but also fleeting. We think of it as something we can fall in and out of, like a puddle of water, and that once it evaporates, we must search for it somewhere else. We view love in terms of making ourselves happy.

The Bible paints a different picture of love.

Love is essentially an act of the will. It is an enduring, unconditional commitment. It is not self-centered; rather, it works for the good and wellbeing of others. *"It always protects, always trusts, always hopes, always perseveres. Love never fails."* (1 Corinthians 13:7-8, NIV)

> "You never lose by loving. You always lose by holding back."
>
> - Barbara de Angelis

While love is often accompanied by deep feelings and emotional attachment, it is not dependent upon those things. In fact, while we tend to think that loving feelings inspire loving actions, the opposite can also be true: loving actions can engender loving feelings.

Whether you're more in love with your wife today than ever or your feelings need recharging, the chapters that follow will give you ideas for communicating love to her in meaningful, practical ways. Nothing on this list is original or particularly profound, but sometimes it's the simple things that turn out to be the most important.

Introduction – Where's the Love?

If, for instance, a husband has routinely spent three or four hours each evening playing video games or surfing the Internet, but then decides to use that time talking with his wife, helping around the house, and playing with the kids instead, the change will definitely be dramatic.

I have attempted to give some concrete examples of how to follow the command to love your neighbor within the context of marriage. Each chapter ends with suggestions for putting into practice what you've learned.

> "Love is not about how much you say 'I love you,' but about how much you prove it's true."
>
> - Author Unknown

Feel free to pick and choose those things that best fit your situation: Eat the meat, spit out the bones. Certainly nothing I have suggested here is written in stone, but the underlying principles definitely are.

I've often told my children that the secret to a happy marriage is to marry someone amazing.

The good news? Your wife *is* amazing!

You were certain of this when you married her, right? If that perspective has blurred somewhat since your wedding day, make it your goal to rediscover the amazing.

But here's the thing to remember: Seeing the amazing doesn't cause you to love her.

Loving her causes you to see the amazing.

Put It into Practice:

✎ Commit Ephesians 5:28-30 to memory and review it often: *"So husbands ought also to love their own wives as their own bodies. He who loves his own wife loves himself; for no one ever hated his own flesh, but nourishes and cherishes it, just as Christ does the church, because we are members of His body."* Make it a priority to live these verses out in your daily life.

✎ Pray that God would open your eyes to your wife's amazing qualities and renew those deep feelings of love for her. More importantly, pray that even in the absence of such feelings, God will strengthen you and give you the willpower to love your wife in the way He has called you to love her, unconditionally and self-sacrificially.

✎ If you are really feeling brave, show this book's table of contents to your wife and ask her to star the chapters she'd like you to work on first. Give every effort to make improvement in those areas, and check back with her at predetermined intervals for a progress report.

Listen

Chapter 1

Have you ever tried to carry on a conversation with someone who is texting on a smartphone at the same time? It can be an exercise in frustration for both parties.

"Hey, someone painted your left eyebrow purple," you might say, just to see if the person is listening.

"Uh-huh," your friend grunts in reply, fingers flying ninety miles a minute across the miniature keyboard.

"Right," you say, knowing full well you are not being heard, "guess I'll catch you later." Eyes still glued to the keypad, your friend gives a barely perceptible head nod as you walk away.

I know a nurse who has a great way of handling this type situation when dealing with a male doctor who won't pay attention. She looks over the doctor's shoulder and says emphatically, "Whoa, look at the figure on that girl!"

The doctor's head invariably whips around in search of the non-existent bombshell. Seeing no one there, he turns back to his nurse in confusion.

"What girl?" he asks, bewildered.

To which the nurse casually replies, "Now that I have your attention, Doctor, I need to ask you about a patient in the ICU."

> "The most basic of all human needs is the need to understand and be understood. The best way to understand people is to listen to them."
>
> - Ralph G. Nichols

Everybody wants to be heard. I think that is why blogging is so popular. The most introverted person can electronically shout their feelings to the world without ever opening their mouth.

I know one young girl who is so painfully shy that she can hardly look a person in the eye, yet she writes very beautiful and insightful blog posts. She has found a way to make her voice heard, and—out there in cyberspace—people are listening.

Have you ever wondered why some women strike up relationships with men in prison whom they've never met? It is simple. The prisoners listen. Those men are literally a captive audience. Whatever the prisoner's motives may be, the women find it intoxicating to have a man in their life who will actually *listen* to what they have to say.

I read a report several years ago that estimated sixty percent of patients who go see the doctor have nothing wrong with them. They just need someone to talk to.

Having spent four years as a general practice physician while training to be an anesthesia specialist, I can attest that this statistic is probably accurate. Many of my patients were very vocal about why they were willing to wait for hours to see me rather than walk right in at a clinic down the street:

"You listen," they'd say. "That's rare in doctors these days."[1]

In fact, I think this is one of the greatest failures of modern medicine—doctors do not really listen. Physicians know a lot about diseases, tests, and medications, but they often neglect one of the most important tools they have at their disposal: their ears!

> "There's a lot of difference between listening and hearing."
>
> - G.K. Chesterton

Unfortunately, husbands often have the same problem as doctors in this area: we have a hard time sitting still and actually listening. Like physicians, husbands want to quickly fix the problem and move on. But not everything in life can be fixed with a pill or a piece of duct tape.

There is a terrific video going around the Internet right now called "It's Not About the Nail."[2] The clip shows a girl with a nail sticking out of her forehead, complaining about a headache to her husband. He, naturally, wants to remove the nail. She just wants to talk about it. The scene really captures the mutual frustration that both men and women feel when trying to communicate with each other.

> "Being heard
> is so close
> to being loved
> that for the average person,
> they are almost
> indistinguishable."
>
> - David Augsburger

Men tend to be task-oriented (fix the problem), while women tend to be relationship-oriented (talk about the problem). The trick for men is not so much to *stop solving problems*, but to *learn to listen well* before they do.

Nine times out of ten, a man will come up with at least one solution before his wife has even finished uttering her first sentence. Ironically, a woman will already know the solution, ninety-nine times out of a hundred, before she ever even opens her mouth!

It's not about the solution. Solutions are easy. Listening is hard.

My father-in-law used to watch a lot of television. He was a little hard of hearing, so he usually kept the volume turned up pretty loud. My wife's mother would sometimes try to talk over the television to tell him something, but instead of muting the program and focusing his attention on her, Dad would just cup his hand around his ear and lean in closer to the set. Rather than tuning out the TV, he tried to tune out his wife!

Although we don't have a television at our house, my wife still catches me "tuning out" occasionally. She'll be in the middle of telling me a story, and I'll be staring off into space, mentally rehashing some event or conversation from earlier in the day. Whether the distractions are internal or external, our wives can easily tell when we're not paying attention.

Calvin Coolidge once said, "It takes a great man to be a good listener." Do you know what? He was right. So how can we learn to listen better? Here are five basic things husbands can do to hone their listening skills:

- **First, minimize distractions.**

    Kids who are being boisterous should be made to settle down or sent to another room. Televisions and radios should be turned down if not turned completely off. Laptops should be closed and cellphones pocketed.

    I'll normally place my phone or tablet facedown on the table beside me in order to physically

> "Most of the successful people I've known are the ones who do more listening than talking."
>
> - Bernard M. Baruch

demonstrate to my wife that she does, indeed, have my full attention.

- **Second, make eye contact.**

  It may feel awkward at first, especially if you are accustomed to staring at your shoes or at the newspaper, but this is essential to letting your wife know you care about what she has to say. Look into her eyes, even if it's hard.

  One of our sons had a difficult time looking people in the eye when he was younger. Even so, we insisted he do it, because we realized his habit of avoiding eye contact would cripple his ability to communicate and might even make him appear untrustworthy.

  With practice, he was able to overcome that unconscious quirk and is now one of the most comfortable, confident, and outgoing young men one could ever hope to meet.

- **Third, give frequent affirmation.**

  Do you get what your wife is saying? Nod your head in understanding. Do you agree? Let her know that. Say positive things like, "Uh-huh" and "I see." These actions will communicate to her that you are paying attention and following her train of thought.

- **Fourth, ask questions.**

  If you don't understand something your wife has just told you, don't pretend like you do.

Instead, ask insightful, intelligent questions. This allows you to clarify any ambiguities in what you think you heard her say (and it also helps her know for sure when she's gotten her point across).

- **Fifth and finally, summarize.**

  Repeat back, in a nutshell, what your wife just told you. This serves to cement what was discussed into your memory and reassures your beloved that she has truly been heard.

Although these five suggestions may seem difficult initially, they will begin to flow more naturally after you've gotten a little practice doing them. Keep it up, and don't grow discouraged. Even if it takes time, your wife will appreciate your earnest efforts to live with her in an understanding way.[3]

> "To be truly heard is the longing of every human heart, and your wife is no exception."
>
> - Doug Flanders

The best part is that, once you really begin to listen, you'll be amazed at what interesting thoughts your wife has to share!

Put It into Practice:

✎ To be truly heard is the longing of every human heart. Set aside some time *every day* to look into your wife's eyes and really listen to what she has to say. You may be surprised at what you hear.

✎ If you must bring your smartphone to the dinner table, leave it in your pocket. Instead of reading emails or sending texts, use that time to connect with your spouse and children, to hear the stories of their day, and to share with them yours.

✎ Commit James 1:19 to memory and pray for grace to live by it: *"This you know, my beloved brethren. But everyone must be quick to hear, slow to speak, and slow to anger."*

✎ "Most people do not listen with the intent to understand," observes Stephen Covey, "they listen with the intent to reply."[4] When talking with your wife, resist the urge to mentally rehearse what you intend to say next. Instead, focus on the words coming out of your wife's mouth, with a sincere desire to understand the thoughts and feelings behind them.

Communicate

Chapter 2

Okay. So now you've minimized distractions. You've made it a habit to look into your wife's eyes and focus on what she's trying to tell you. You've taken time to listen, and she's undoubtedly noticed the change.

But when it comes to communication, listening is only half of the equation. Don't make your wife guess what you are thinking or feeling. She longs for you to open up and let her in. Won't you share your heart with her?

Those hopes and dreams that fuel your work and energize your efforts? She wants to know about them.

The worries or concerns that nag at your thoughts and disrupt your sleep? She'd like to hear those, too, so that she'll better be able to comfort and support and encourage you through them—and so she can sympathize and strategize and pray with you over them.

Your wife would love to linger over a cup of coffee in conversation with you. Or if coffee's not her thing, make her a cup of hot tea, or take her out for a milkshake. Good communication is vital to maintaining a strong and healthy marriage relationship, so set aside a little time every day when the two of you can check in with each other and make that important connection.

> "Communication is a skill that you can learn. It's like riding a bicycle or typing. If you're willing to work at it, you can rapidly improve the quality of every part of your life."
>
> - Brian Tracy

If you are not used to communicating with your wife in this fashion, it may feel a little awkward at first, but don't give up! Keep working at it. Carve out time consistently for it. And your relationship will deepen and improve as a result.

If this all sounds good, but you don't know where to begin, here is a short list of conversation starters to get you going.

Chapter 2 – Communicate

Try one of these, and see where it leads you:

- "You'll never believe what happened at work today…."

- "I heard something funny on the radio this morning…."

- "I'm really enjoying this book. Let me read you what it says here about…."

- "Did anything interesting come in the mail or email today?"

- "I have this weekend off—is there anything special you'd like to do?"

- "I plan to walk around the block after dinner. Do you want to join me?"

If it's hard for you to remember the things that happen during the day that you'd like to share with your wife when you get back home, try jotting little notes to yourself to serve as a reminder. I often keep such a running list in my pocket, then refer to it in the evening once I've been reunited with my family.

> "Communication works for those who work at it."
>
> - John Powell

Alternatively, you could text teasers to your wife throughout the day: "Remind me to tell you about something funny that just happened once I get home."

That works, too.

Later, when you're sitting face-to-face with your wife over that cup of coffee, share with her those stories in detail. Take your time. More than just imparting factual information, your wife wants to know what you think about it. How you're feeling. She'll probably try to read between the lines regardless, but if you don't give her enough lines to work with, she'll likely wind up with some faulty conclusions, so don't hold back.

Once you've finished running through your little list of stuff to tell her, don't get in too big a hurry to mark "daily communication" off your to-do list and move on. Give her an opportunity to open up, too.

Don't forget to practice those listening skills!

If she senses your impatience, she'll hesitate, so refill your cups and give her your undivided attention. Ask open-ended questions—things that can't be answered with a simple "yes" or "no."

If she is happy about something, rejoice with her. If she's sad, offer a shoulder to cry on. If she's excited, show enthusiasm. If she's upset, hear her out.

> "Any problem, big or small, within a family, always seems to start with bad communication. Someone isn't listening."
>
> - Emma Thompson

Do your best to look at things from her perspective. Sympathize with her and avoid passing judgment.

Try not to rush to a solution if she isn't asking for one. If you are thoughtful about it, you can often lead her to the solution through your questions and continued interest in a way that doesn't make her feel like you're just trying to fix things fast to shut her up.

Chapter 2 – Communicate

Whenever you are discussing areas of conflict or disagreement, be honest with your wife, but not brutally so. Be gentle. Always and only *speak the truth in love.*[1]

Some people are so concerned with communicating TRUTH that they completely forget to do so in LOVE. Such communication is overly harsh and usually ineffective.

Others are so intent on communicating LOVE that they willingly compromise or suppress the TRUTH to do it. This is shortsighted and misguided—and is ultimately not very loving, either.

We desperately need to strike a balance between the two, and only wisdom from above will help us do that. Fortunately for us, God promises to grant wisdom to all who ask.[2]

Every verbal exchange you have with your wife has the potential to knit your hearts closer together. Even difficult discussions can be handled in a way that ultimately achieves that goal, but it won't happen by accident. In order for this to happen, thought must be given not only to the words that are said, but also to the tone and attitude and body language that accompany those words.

> "Good words are worth much, and cost little."
>
> - George Herbert

Learning to communicate well takes time and practice—but isn't having a healthy marriage and happy wife worth the investment?

Put It into Practice:

✍ If you are not used to communicating with your wife at a deeper level, you may feel a little vulnerable when you try. Start anyway, and stick with it. Work at it little by little, sharing more and more each day, until doing so feels second nature.

✍ Make a list of things you would like to be able to discuss with your wife. Pray about your list, and set aside time for those conversations—during a dinner date alone or over early morning coffee or on a quiet stroll in the cool of the evening.

✍ Make a habit of connecting with your wife daily. Talk, listen, converse. Remove all other distractions (or, in the case of children, incorporate them into the conversation, as well).

✍ If you are separated from your wife during the day, carry an index card in your pocket (or a smart phone with a note-making app) to jot down things you think of during the day that you want to remember to tell your wife and/or kids in the evening.

Sing Her
Praises

Chapter 3

The people at the hospital where I work undoubtedly get tired of hearing me brag about my wife, but one thing is certain: They know how I feel about her. There is no question in their mind that I love her dearly and am 100% devoted to her.

A husband who can't find a kind word to spare about his spouse is shooting himself in the foot. Badmouthing your wife reflects more poorly on you than on the woman you married.

Do you want to strengthen your marriage and make your wife feel loved? Then shamelessly brag about her good qualities and quietly pray about her bad ones. Her reputation is your reputation.

It may be human nature to voice our criticisms and withhold our praise—we do it with our children, our coworkers, and our spouses alike—but that's not the way to build a happy, healthy home. Praise is every bit as important, if not more so, than the vast majority of our alleged "constructive criticisms."

> "The praise that comes from love does not make us vain, but more humble."
>
> - James M. Barrie

But how can we do better? How do we change bad habits?

To unlock the power of praise, the first step is to seek things that can be praised. We must train our eyes to focus on the good instead of searching out the bad.

Sometimes this is easy. Your spouse may be physically beautiful or musically talented or obviously outstanding in any number of ways. If so, she may already receive regular praise, not only from you, but from many around her.

But whether we have such praiseworthy qualities or not, these are not the areas where we most desperately seek affirmation.

Rather it is in areas of character, wisdom, and diligence that we most desire recognition. It is in the areas over which we have a measure of control that praise is most meaningful.

If these things are harder to spot, it is only because we are not accustomed to looking for them. However, once we begin to seek, we discover that they are readily found.

Chapter 3 – Sing Her Praises

View it as a treasure hunt. See how many virtuous qualities you can identify in your wife's life and actions, then praise them accordingly:

- Is your wife truthful? Commend her honesty and integrity. Praise her for being principled.

- Is your wife hard-working? Praise her diligence and initiative. Thank her for all she does to keep your home running smoothly.

- Is your wife a good mother? Acknowledge her patience with the children and the tender love with which she cares for them.

> "Love is a gross exaggeration of the difference between one person and everybody else.
>
> - George Bernard Shaw

- Does your wife cook for you? Praise her for that, even (especially) if she's "culinarily challenged." Thank her for the time and effort she puts into preparing nutritious and/or delicious meals for your family.

- Does your wife take care of her appearance? Let her know how much you appreciate that. Notice and compliment her new dress or shoes or hairstyle. Show her you (still) find her attractive, and tell her why. Be specific!

- Is your wife compassionate toward others? Praise her kindness, thoughtfulness, and generosity. Encourage her to use her gifts for God's glory.

- Is your wife a bargain hunter? Praise her thrift and resourcefulness. Thank her for being careful in how she spends money.

- Is your wife artistically, athletically, or musically gifted? Admire her abilities and encourage their continued development.

Even your wife's negative behavior can sometimes signal the presence of positive character qualities:

- Is she a little nit-picky? Praise her attention to detail and pray about how you might help her channel it in a more constructive way.

- Does she harbor grudges? Then she probably has a good memory! Try to help her recall and focus on the good rather than the bad. Teach her to memorize and meditate on Scripture.

- Is she overly sensitive? That may mean she has a deep capacity for empathy. Pray that God would open her eyes to the hurts and hardships of others and would use your wife to address those needs.

- Is she plagued with self-doubt? Praise her humility, even as you seek to build her up in Christ.

Not only should you praise your wife to her face, but you should also speak highly of her behind her back.

Follow the example we read in Proverbs:

"The sweetest
of all sounds
is praise."

- Xenophon

"Her children arise and call her blessed; her husband also, and he praises her, saying: 'Many women do noble things, but you surpass them all.'" (Proverbs 31:28-29, NIV)

19

Put It into Practice:

✎ Keep a running list of all the things you admire and appreciate about your wife. Refer to it often and be liberal in your praise of her, both when directing comments to her and when you are talking to others.

✎ If you find yourself in the company of men who are speaking ill of their wives, don't be tempted to commiserate. While that might not be the best time to launch into a recitation of all your wife's good qualities, do see if you can guide the conversation in a more positive direction and encourage the other husbands to search out and focus on their own wife's good points.

✎ Don't wait until your wife is feeling down to praise and encourage her. Build her up every chance you get. Send her a text during the day praising her and thanking her for specific qualities.

✎ Next time you find yourself getting irritated by something your wife says or does, look for a positive trait that she may be misusing. Praise her for *that*, then gently and prayerfully direct her toward ways of exercising her strengths more constructively.

Pray for/with Her

Chapter 4

My wife and I made a deal when we were first married that we have faithfully kept for more than a quarter of a century now: we agreed to always stop and pray together before being physically intimate.

We thought that by linking something we knew we *should* do with something we knew we *would* do, we'd get two good habits for the price of one.

Little did we realize at the time, but that was one of the best decisions we ever made in terms of building a strong, stable, and healthy marriage. This commitment ensured that we were not only becoming physically one, but we were becoming spiritually one, as well.

As it turns out, spiritual intimacy is even more important than physical intimacy in terms of marriage longevity. Praying alongside your wife will strengthen your relationship like nothing else. Studies show that couples who regularly pray together stay together, enjoying less than a one percent divorce rate compared to the usual fifty-plus percent among Christians and non-Christians alike.[1]

This makes sense, of course, when you think about it. For starters, regular prayer is an indication that you take your beliefs seriously. Your faith isn't just some cultural tradition that you have adopted from your parents or society; it's something more than an intellectual exercise in which you participate each Sunday.

> "To be a Christian without prayer is no more possible than to be alive without breathing."
>
> - Martin Luther

If you pray regularly, it means you really believe in a personal and powerful God who can hear your prayers, who cares about their content, and who has the strength and goodness to respond appropriately.

Furthermore, it stands to reason that if you believe in that kind of God, you are going to take the marriage vows you made before Him very seriously. When you pray as a couple, you acknowledge God's vital role in the success of your marriage. Not only is every beat of your heart and every breath of your lungs a gift from Him, but so is every single day of your marriage.

Chapter 4 – Pray for/with Her

God invented marriage. He invented physical intimacy. He invented babies. He loves these things.

Over and over in Scripture, God compares His relationship with us to that of the marital union between a husband and wife. Surely if God loves marriage, He will help all who seek His face in prayer and ask for His strength and wisdom in building up and preserving their marriage.

> "Any concern too small to be turned into a prayer is too small to be made into a burden."
>
> - Corrie Ten Boom

If you've not already done so, get in the habit of praying with your wife every day. I would encourage you to associate your joint prayer times with something you already do together regularly. This will provide a natural reminder and will make it easier for you to integrate prayer into your daily routine.

Although linking prayer to times of physical intimacy has worked out well for my wife and me, you are certainly not obligated to follow suit. You may prefer, instead, to pray together first thing in the morning, or at mealtimes, or before bed each night.

It doesn't matter when you pray, only that you pray, and that you do so together.

In addition to praying *with* your wife, however, I encourage you to faithfully pray *for* her, as well. Praying on your wife's behalf not only enlists the help of the Almighty, but also puts her and her needs at the forefront of your heart and mind, right where they belong. One simple and easy method of doing this is by praying for your wife from head to toe....

- **Pray for Her Brain:**

  Pray that God would mold her into a capable, intelligent, and virtuous woman and would keep her thoughts centered on whatever is true, lovely, right, pure, noble, and worthy of praise. (Proverbs 31:10; Philippians 4:8)

- **Pray for Her Eyes:**

  Ask God to give her eyes of compassion, so she could see others as He sees them. (Matthew 9:36; 1 Samuel 16:7b)

- **Pray for Her Ears:**

  Pray that she would listen for God's still, small voice and would remain ever attentive to His promptings. (Matthew 11:15; 1 Thessalonians 5:19)

- **Pray for Her Mouth:**

  Ask that God would fill her mouth with skillful and godly wisdom, that the law of kindness would remain on her tongue, and that she would only and always speak the truth in love. (Proverbs 31:26; Ephesians 4:15)

- **Pray for Her Heart:**

  Pray that God would fill your wife's heart with love and respect for you and with tender patience toward your children. (Ephesians 5:33; 1 Thessalonians 2:7)

- **Pray for Her Arms:**

  Ask God to gird your wife with strength, making her arms strong and firm. Pray that He would bless the labor of her hands and would enable her to do all her work cheerfully, as unto Him. (Colossians 3:23; Proverbs 31:17, 31)

- **Pray for Her Womb:**

  Pray that God would bless the fruit of her womb by giving her children who walk in truth. (3 John 1:4; Psalm 127:3)

- **Pray for Her Legs:**

  Ask God to strengthen and sustain your wife, so that she can walk and not faint, nor tire of doing good. (2 Thessalonians 3:13; Isaiah 40:31)

- **Pray for Her Feet:**

  Pray that her feet would be shod with the preparation of the gospel of peace so that she might faithfully pursue righteousness and love. Ask God to lead her in the path of wisdom and truth and to keep her foot from stumbling. (Proverbs 4:11-12; 21:21; Ephesians 6:15)

"Father, bless our marriage With long and loving years. Help us seek your will for life, Through happy days and tears.... We know our love will stay alive— Your Word says this is true— If we join our hearts together, And lift them up to You!"

- Sue Skeen

Put It into Practice:

✍ Commit to praying with your wife every day.[2] This is one of the best things you can do for the strength and longevity of your marriage, so make it a priority.

✍ Print Philippians 4:6 on an index card or sticky note, place it in a prominent place in your home, and then commit it to memory, especially if either (or both) you or your wife are prone to worry: *"Be anxious for nothing, but in everything by prayer and supplication with thanksgiving let your requests be made known to God."* (Philippians 4:6, NASB) Purpose to make the keeping of this command a lifelong habit.

✍ As the Lord blesses you with children, incorporate them into family prayer times—especially when praying over big decisions that will affect their future. Encourage them to pray aloud with the family and individually during their times of personal devotion.

Value Her
Individuality

Chapter 5

Your wife is wonderfully unique. Don't compare her to your mom, or your ex-wife, or your old girlfriend. Your mom may make the best chocolate chip cookies in the world, but unfavorable comparisons won't win you brownie points!

Try to appreciate your wife for who she is, and don't attempt to force her into the mold of what you think she should be. God alone can change anything in her that needs changing. Your efforts to do so will fall flat or backfire.

Men and women tend to view the world from dissimilar perspectives. Please understand: Just because your wife approaches things in a different way than you, does not mean her way is *wrong*. It's just *different*.

Women, for example, are usually more emotionally sensitive than men and also better able to read and interpret facial expressions. They tend to be more nurturing by nature, and are often more verbal, as well. Those are all good things!

You shouldn't view such strengths and differences as a threat. Learn, instead, to value your wife's individuality *and* her input (more on that topic in Chapter 23).

My wife likes classical music, and I like classic rock. She eats lots of fruits and vegetables; I eat meat, meat, and more meat. She tends to be more formal, and I'm a little more laid back.

> "If everyone is thinking alike, then no one is thinking."
>
> -Benjamin Franklin

Our life goals, however, are the same: building a marriage that glorifies God, raising our children to love and serve Him, and encouraging other husbands and wives to put their spouse's needs ahead of their own.

Recognize the fact that God matched you up with your wife for good reason. She is undoubtedly weak in some areas where you are strong, but the reverse is also true: Your wife is strong in some areas where you are weak. You need to appreciate this fact and use it to your mutual advantage!

This book is a perfect example of such synergy.

Chapter 5 – Value Her Individuality

I am great at coming up with ideas, but since my medical practice keeps me at the hospital 80 hours a week, I don't have time to flesh out very many of those ideas or see them to completion.

Fortunately, God gave me a woman who is very good at putting meat on my bones (in more ways than one!).

I was able to dictate much of the text you are now reading while our family was on an extended road trip. My wife typed while I drove. Once we got home, she edited, polished, and formatted that text into the volume you now hold in your hands.

"The things that make me different are the things that make me me."

-A.A. Milne

You would be wise to look for such common ground with your own wife—ways in which you and she can work together, both using your unique skills, talents, aptitudes, and abilities for the glory of God and for the good of your family, your church, and your community.

Put It into Practice:

✍ Think about the things that originally attracted you to your wife. Were they areas in which she was very similar to you or areas in which you were different? Ask God to renew your love and appreciation for your wife's differences.

✍ Have you been guilty of trying to change your wife or mold her into something God may never have intended her to be? If so, repent of your wrong attitude. Confess and seek forgiveness. Leave any changes that need to be made to God, and trust Him to mature you both. *"He who began a good work in you will be faithful to complete it."* (Philippians 1:6, NASB)

✍ Memorize Philippians 4:8, *"Whatever is true, whatever is honorable, whatever is right, whatever is pure, whatever is lovely, whatever is of good repute, if there is any excellence and if anything worthy of praise, dwell on these things."* Pray that God will help you to focus on and value all those things that are good, right, lovely, and praiseworthy in your wife.

✍ Referring to the lists you made in Chapter 3, thank God for your wife's various strengths. Ask Him to give you wisdom to know how those strengths might best be utilized for the good of others and His own glory.

Don't
Leave the
Seat Up

Chapter 6

Put the seat down. Perpetually raised toilet seats are a pet peeve of wives everywhere. And while you're at it, tidy up a bit.

Bathroom etiquette is really just a specific example of the general principle of thoughtfulness. It's an opportunity to apply the admonition we find in Philippians 2:6—

> *"Do not merely look out for your own personal interests, but also for the interests of others."*

In every relationship, thoughtful consideration goes a long way toward keeping things amicable. This is no less true in a marriage than in any other association.

Getting the door for your wife, helping her with her coat, carrying heavy loads for her—such small acts of kindness will assure her that you care and will demonstrate (as in the case of lowering the toilet seat) that you are thinking of her, even when she isn't present.

> "He who
> is faithful in a
> very little thing
> is faithful also
> in much."
>
> - Luke 16:10

Such niceties prove that pleasing her in little ways—both in public and in private—is important to you.

Putting a seat back into position may seem like a small and insignificant thing, but it serves as a bellwether for being considerate in other, more important areas, as well. Your wife knows that if you faithfully tend to this very minor thing, she can count on you to take care of the more significant stuff, too.

Legend has it that the band Van Halen used to make a very unusual demand in all their performance contracts.[1] Buried deep within the long lists of technical requirements would be instructions that a bowl full of M&Ms, with all the brown candies removed, should be left on the lead singer's dressing table before the concert. If a band member found so much as a single brown M&M backstage, it would nullify the contract and give the band legal grounds to cancel the scheduled performance.

There was a practical purpose behind this seemingly capricious contract clause: It let the band know how closely all the other legalese had been read. If the brown-free bowl of M&Ms was in its proper place,

Van Halen could be fairly certain that the concert promoters had also attended to the more significant matters, such as weight, wattage, safety, and structural specifications that, if ignored, might spell damage, disaster, or even death for performers and patrons alike.

If the candy clause were marginalized or ignored, it caused them to question what other, more important things had been missed or disregarded. They would therefore perform a more detailed line check themselves and, if necessary, cancel the concert altogether.

With respect to husbands and toilet seats, thoughtful attention to this minor detail also demonstrates the fact that, although you might intrinsically care about different things, you are willing to accommodate your wife in this way, because you understand that it's important to her.

> "It's the little details that are vital. Little things make big things happen."
>
> - John Wooden

Men and women are different. Sometimes things that are extremely important to one don't matter at all to the other. You wouldn't want your wife to disregard the things that mean a lot to you, so don't do the same to her.

Want to store up a little good will for yourself? Then treat your spouse as you wish to be treated—even in matters as seemingly insignificant as toilet seats.

Put It into Practice:

✍ Are you already in the habit of putting the seat down? If so, keep up the good work! If not, make a conscious effort to show consideration to your wife in this area.

✍ Have you allowed certain other niceties to slip since your dating years? Show your wife that chivalry is not dead. Get her door. Hold her coat. Offer your arm as you walk together. What are some other small ways you can demonstrate your love to her?

✍ Ask your wife to identify any blind spots. Is there something you're unconsciously doing that she finds annoying? If so, address it and do your best to establish better habits going forward. I know, for instance, that my wife doesn't like for me to drive without a seatbelt. I could go for miles without ever noticing the little car alarm that riding beltless sets off, but listening to it chime every 90-seconds really drives her batty, even if she's just hearing it in the background when I phone her on my way home from work. Knowing this, I've made a concerted effort to strap in more regularly—especially when she's riding in the car with me.

Throw Dirty
Clothes in
the Hamper

Chapter 7

God designed your wife to be your helpmeet, but that doesn't mean she's your slave. Be careful not to treat her like one. Pitch in to help around the house, rather than expecting her to tidy up all your messes.

Don't leave your dirty clothes scattered on the floor. More than likely, the hamper is only a few steps away from wherever you are dropping them anyway. Make this a habit, and it will let your wife know that you don't consider her your personal maid or cleanup crew.

As a husband, God has given you work to do, both in your family, in your church, and in your community. He has provided you with a wife to help carry out those duties, so be appreciative and don't take her for granted.

Whether you think of her as an assistant manager, an assistant coach, or your second-in-command, the implication is one of inter-dependence and shared responsibility, not of master and servant. Both husband and wife, in fact, are called to serve and defer to the other. It goes both ways:

- *"Rather, serve one another humbly in love."* (Galatians 5:13b, NIV)

- *"Submit to one another out of reverence for Christ."* (Ephesians 5:21, NIV)

- *"Use whatever gift you have received to serve others, as faithful stewards of God's grace...."* (1 Peter 4:10, NIV)

This is one of my frustrations with the Patriarchal movement: It is sometimes used to cast women in the light of second-class citizens. By no means is this God's design.[1] According to 1 Peter 3:7, our wives are our coworkers and coheirs in Christ, and we are to treat them with honor and respect and are to live with them in an understanding way.[2]

> "Gird yourselves with humility, to serve one another."
>
> - 1 Peter 5:5, ASV

A husband is called to *lead* his family (more on that in Chapter 10), not to be a dictator or tyrant.

As leaders in our homes, we have the privilege, but also the responsibility, of setting the tone and direction for our families. The tone should not be one of selfishness, laziness, or entitlement, but rather, we should be working together to serve Christ and serve our fellow man. Such service should begin at home.

Jesus washed the disciples feet, not the other way around. By Christ's own testimony, He came *"not to be served, but to serve."*[3]

> "The Son of Man did not come to be served, but to serve, and to give His life as a ransom for many."
>
> - Matthew 20:28, NIV

When you are humbly following Christ's selfless example, His love will shine through you, not only to your family, but to everyone who enters your home.

So go ahead. Take out the trash. Help with the dishes. Change an occasional diaper. Throw the dirty clothes in the hamper, and maybe even start a load of laundry.

Your wife could use a helping hand… and doing such things will communicate your love for her on a whole new level.

Put It into Practice:

✎ If you *really* want to show love to your wife, tackle some of the items on her Honey-Do List. Start with the ones you've neglected the longest.

✎ Husbands and wives often hold to different standards of cleanliness. If your wife is the more particular of the two, do your best to follow her standards when helping out with chores. If you tend to be more obsessive-compulsive in this area than she is, then try to help out in a way that doesn't communicate, "You've been doing a slip-shod job. Let me show you how this *should* be done."

✎ Give your wife an even bigger break by teaching your kids to pitch in with the chores, as well.

✎ Still having trouble getting those dirty clothes inside the hamper? That may be because your hamper is inconveniently located. Just as you station trash bins where they'll most likely be needed (in the kitchen, the bathrooms, and beside your desk), it makes sense to store laundry hampers wherever your family is inclined to pull their clothes off. It's okay to have more than one set. We keep hampers in the master bathroom, in each child's bedroom or closet, plus an extra set beside our backdoor for all the dirty socks our children shed there. By having two in each location (one marked "lights" and the other "darks"), the clothes get sorted as we go, and it's a simple matter of emptying the hamper into the washing machine once it gets full.

Turn Off
the TV

Chapter 8

Turn off the TV. Lay aside the video games, pocket the iPhone, and shut off the computer, as well. It is staggering how many hours we waste gazing at some sort of screen, instead of interacting with the real people in our lives.

We're all familiar with the scene: A roomful of teens intently staring at their phones, seemingly unaware that anyone else is present. Don't let that be the status quo in your home with your family.

Consciously set limits on your tube-time, whatever form it takes. Use the time saved to invest in your spouse and children. Take a walk with your wife or play a board game together instead.

Every year, more and more of our free time is being syphoned away by increasingly addictive forms of entertainment: First, there was television. Then the Internet. Now we have Facebook, YouTube, Twitter, and Pinterest. With new social media venues sprouting up almost daily, it is impossible to even keep track of them all, much less stay active on their sites.

We hardly have time left anymore for real people and real relationships. It can stir up feelings of isolation and extreme loneliness, even when we're surrounded by a room full of people.

Here's the problem this situation poses for marriage: You cannot love your wife the way she needs to be loved when your eyes are glued to a screen. She needs you to really be *present,* both physically and mentally. She needs you to be fully engaged in the moment. She needs you to look deep into her eyes and invest your time and energy into your relationship with her.

> "You cannot love your wife the way she needs to be loved when your eyes are glued to a screen."
>
> - Doug Flanders

Nodding your head absentmindedly while you are absorbed in YouTube videos or strategizing your next *World of Warcraft* move or checking online stock quotes does not qualify as quality time. (Nor is meaningful conversation possible while your wife is updating her Facebook status or scrolling through her Twitter newsfeed or pinning all the latest recipes, crafts, and fashions to her Pinterest boards.)

Sometimes, we just need to unplug!

I'm not suggesting that you toss all your technology in the trash. Computers and smart phones can be useful tools when used wisely. But if you are not careful, they will completely take over your life and squeeze out everything—and everyone—else.

There is nothing wrong with watching an occasional television program or taking in a movie together. When chosen with discretion, such forms of entertainment

> "Television has proved that people will look at anything rather than each other."
>
> - Ann Landers

can be a fun and enjoyable way to relax and can provide interesting topics for discussion afterwards.

Just don't allow movie watching or Internet surfing to become the default setting for how you spend all your free time, or you will miss out on some of the best things life has to offer, not the least of which is a closer, healthier, more loving relationship with your wife and children.

Put It into Practice:

✍ Make a list of tech-free things you and your wife can do together for fun (besides the obvious). You might take up a new hobby, train for a 10K, go window shopping, or volunteer at the local soup kitchen. Need more ideas? Check out the list in Chapter 13.

✍ Next time you feel like plopping down in front of the television set, discuss all those wonderful options above, pick one, and go for it. Revisit the list later, when you're ready for a new challenge or adventure.

✍ If you and your wife do decide to watch a movie together, let her choose what you watch every once in awhile. Seeing an occasional chick-flick won't kill you—and it will probably put her in a more romantic mood than that explosive new action/adventure film you had in mind.

✍ Set aside some time *every day*—for an hour or so, at least—to shut down all the screens and connect with one another. No phones. No laptops. No tablets. Just the two of you, together again.

✍ Consider periodically taking longer technology fasts—say, for one day a week, one weekend a month, and/or one week a year. This is especially helpful when you find yourself devoting so much time to television or computer screens that you can't keep up with other responsibilities.

Loosen the
Purse Strings

Chapter 9

We all have to keep an eye on our budget, but an occasional splurge can be well worth it. Seemingly frivolous things like flowers, jewelry, and candlelight dinners let your wife know that she is more valuable to you than a number in your bank account.

The old adage, "You can't take it with you," is as true now as it ever was. Not only that, but it is becoming increasingly in vogue among the uber-rich to leave their wealth to charity rather than to their children—the thought being that smart kids won't need the money and foolish ones will squander it.

We should all save for a rainy day, but there's a balance between being money-wise and being miserly. Not everything a business invests in is practical. Much of it is aesthetic. A two star hotel and a five star hotel both have clean sheets and functional plumbing, but oh, what a difference between the two! The turned-down bed, plush cotton robes, chocolate mints on the pillow—none of these things are essential, but they sure make your stay more pleasant and memorable.

Do what you can to make your marriage a five-star operation. Give attention to those little extras that make your wife feel pampered and appreciated.

You'd think that during lean economic times, sales for stuff like candy, cosmetics, and movie tickets would plummet, right?

Well, that's not the way it has traditionally worked. Those industries have long been dubbed "depression proof." It seems that small luxuries serve to buoy the spirit and give us hope—or at least remind us of better times.

As men, we are often tempted to be practical about everything, but sometimes the most practical thing is to be a little impractical. Sometimes things that seem frivolous to us can be the most important things of all to the ones we love.

> "This idea of selfishness as a virtue, as opposed to generosity: That, to me, is unnatural."
>
> – Jessica Lange

Our family has a neighbor who was two years old when she and her parents were put in a prison camp by the Japanese during WWII.[1] They went into the camp with nothing but the clothes on their backs, but upon their release several years later our neighbor carried with her a prized possession she has kept and cherished ever since—a ragdoll her mother made for her fifth birthday, fashioned from bits of fabric and yarn and stuffing the other prisoners had donated to the cause, each one contributing what they could to give this young girl a glimpse of happiness, even amid such dire circumstances. In reality, the doll was little more than a few threadbare scraps sewn together by loving hands, but it was imbued with such tenderness and *hope* as to make it worth far more than the sum of its parts.

This story goes to show that those little luxuries that so brighten the lives of our loved ones don't have to cost a lot. They just require a little time, thought, and effort, plus a bit of intentionality.

Fresh flowers or dinner out may not be the best thing for the bottom line, but might be the best thing for your marriage. What's more, you can reap the benefits without breaking the bank, since the wildflowers you gather for free in an abandoned field will often work just as well as that store-bought bouquet of long-stemmed roses. And a simple picnic of fruit, sandwiches, and cold lemonade, when served with love, can surpass the most scrumptious gourmet delicacies the priciest restaurant in town has to offer.[2]

> "Happiness is not a luxury. It is a necessity. When we are happy, we are in the best possible place to be good to ourselves and to those we love."
>
> – Suze Orman

Put It into Practice:

✍ Aerin Lauder once said, "Luxury is anything that feels special. I mean, it can be a moment, it can be a walk on the beach, it could be a kiss from your child, or it could be a beautiful picture frame, a special fragrance. I think luxury doesn't necessarily have to mean expensive." Ask your wife to make a list of the things that make her feel special, then incorporate as many as you can into your day-to-day lives.

✍ There are some things in life—music, art, and sports, to name a few—we enjoy, but aren't about making money. There's money to be made in such fields, to be sure, but the majority of us do them simply for the joy and pleasure inherent in the doing. Many men have no problem making time for sports, but things like art and music aren't even on their radar. They should be. Listening to beautiful music as you relax around the house, hanging beautiful artwork on the walls of your home—such things can enrich your life if you choose styles you and your wife both enjoy.

✍ Remember, it's the thought that counts: For 27 years, I've worn a wedding band that originally cost $86. Were I to pawn it, I'd be lucky to get half that today. The ring's value lies not in its monetary worth, but in its symbolism. The same holds true for many of the ways I pamper my wife: making her a cup of hot tea, running her bath water, bringing her chocolate kisses from the grocery store—these things cost pennies, but count for far more. What small investments pay the biggest dividends in your marriage?

Practice Servant-Leadership

Chapter 10

All organizations have a hierarchy. It is impossible to function well without one. But being a leader isn't the same as being a dictator. The best role model is Jesus Christ, not Joseph Stalin.

Although it's a challenge to exercise authority while maintaining a spirit of humility, that is what being a godly leader entails. Jesus washed his disciples feet, then died on their behalf. Husbands are called to love their wives in the same self-sacrificing way:

- *"Husbands, love your wives, just as Christ loved the church and gave himself up for her to make her holy, cleansing her*

> *by the washing with water through the word."* (Ephesians 5:25-26, NASB)

- *"Anyone who wants to be first must be the very last, and the servant of all."* (Mark 9:35, NIV)

- *"Have this attitude in yourselves which was also in Christ Jesus, who, although He existed in the form of God, did not regard equality with God a thing to be grasped, but emptied Himself, taking the form of a bond-servant...."* (Philippians 2:5-7, NASB)

The best leaders exhibit several qualities: They are transparent; they expect as much or more of themselves as of those they're attempting to lead; and they put the good of the organization (or, in the case of a husband-leader, the good of the family) ahead of their own interests or any personal gain.

> "Love does not dominate; it cultivates."
>
> – Johann Wolfgang von Goethe

Let's look at each of these three qualities in closer detail:

1 **First and foremost, a servant-leader is transparent.** Transparency implies there are no hidden agendas. Everyone is on the same team, working toward the same goals, and those goals are clearly defined and understood. Transparency means honesty, fairness, forthrightness, and above all, accountability.

Transparency with a spouse can be difficult. Some things are hard to talk about with anybody, let alone with someone we care about, someone of the opposite gender, someone whose admiration and respect we so deeply crave.

A good rule of thumb is, if you'd be uncomfortable discussing it afterward with your wife, then you probably shouldn't be doing it in the first place.

Of course, personality differences can make even innocent discussions more difficult than they should be—I dreaded telling my sentimental wife when I recently traded in an old Ford truck she loved for two small economy cars, even though it made good financial sense to do so—but that isn't what I'm talking about here.

> "A good rule of thumb is, if you would be uncomfortable discussing it afterward with your wife, then you probably shouldn't be doing it in the first place."
>
> – Doug Flanders

When it comes to being transparent with our children, that can be hard, too, but it is important that they know our weaknesses as well as our strengths, our failures as well as our victories. Because our kids share our humanity as well as our genes, their weaknesses will often mirror our own, and they'll benefit from hearing how we've overcome various struggles. There is no need to go into great detail about your failings, but don't pretend you are without faults.

A servant-leader is quick to accept blame, apologize, and ask forgiveness whenever the situation warrants it. And he understands the importance of maintaining a clear conscience and therefore strives to behave in a way—both publicly and privately—that is honorable, dependable, and above reproach.

2 Second, a servant-leader is not above the law.

Nor does he *consider* himself above the law. The US Congress provides a classic example of the opposite of this principle, routinely passing bad legislation from which the lawmakers themselves are exempt.

With a true servant-leader, there is no such hypocrisy. The rules are applied equally to all. He expects as much or more of himself as of the people he leads, for he knows that as their leader, he will incur a stricter judgment.[1]

> "The quality of a leader is reflected in the standards they set for themselves."
>
> – Ray Kroc

The father who smokes two packs a day, but warns his kids to never take up the habit? He is doing neither himself nor his children nor his health any favors.

I may not struggle with hypocrisy in such an obvious way as this, yet I sometimes expect things of my wife and children that I am unwilling or unable to do myself:

- I want them to hear me out, although I often interrupt
- I expect them to be patient and thoughtful and self-controlled, even when I haven't been.
- I would like for them to look their best, even if I skip shaving or look a little shabby myself.
- I want them to control their emotions and refrain from pouting, crying, or acting moody in any way, yet sometimes I fail to control the temper that provokes such moodiness, sulkiness, and tears.

And I do all these things, despite the fact that the Word of God repeatedly warns against such behavior:

> "A leader is one who knows the way, goes the way, and shows the way."
>
> – John C. Maxwell

- *"Let love be without hypocrisy. Abhor what is evil; cling to what is good."*(Romans 12:9, NASB)

- *"[Love] does not act unbecomingly; it does not seek its own, is not provoked, does not take into account a wrong suffered, does not rejoice in unrighteousness, but rejoices with the truth...."* (1 Corinthians 13:5-6, NASB)

- *"Fathers, do not provoke your children to anger, but bring them up in the discipline and instruction of the Lord."* (Ephesians 6:4, NASB)

The take-home message? We need to *be* and *do* the things we want our wives and children to *be* and *do*.

We should expect as much or more of ourselves as we do of them. We must lead by example.

3 **Third, a servant-leader thinks of others first.**
He puts the good of the organization ahead of his own needs or personal advantage. He leads selflessly and sacrificially. He considers the interests of others as more important than his own.[2]

I've known both styles of leaders: Those who use the organization to serve themselves, and those who use themselves to serve the organization.

> "Leadership should be born out of an understading of the needs of those who would be affected by it."
>
> – Marian Anderson

Although I've crossed paths with a few embezzlers over the years, embezzlement is not the only way to steal from a company. It's just the most obvious way.

Many people manipulate vacation schedules, work assignments, and tax credits to their own benefit. They are always watching out for number one, always looking for loopholes. Whatever will garner the best perks or put the most money in their pocket with the least amount of effort is what they will do, every time—whether it's ethical or not.

A servant-leader is the opposite. He does what is best for those he serves, even when it requires personal sacrifice to do so. For the family man, this may mean driving mini-vans instead of sports cars, going on family vacations instead of golfing excursions, living in a modest home in suburbia instead of a high-rise apartment in the city, or getting braces for Junior instead of a new flat-screen TV.

The term "servant-leader" is what Buddhists would call a *koan*—a seemingly contradictory statement that forces a person to stop and think more deeply about a subject, so as to bring about an even greater enlightenment.

Yet leaders *should* serve those they lead. The only reason servant-leadership seems like a koan or an oxymoron to our society today is because we have grown so accustomed to leaders who abuse their power and use it to benefit themselves, often to the detriment of the people they are supposed to represent.

> "A servant-leader strives to behave in a way— both publicly and privately— that is honorable, dependable, and above reproach."
>
> – Doug Flanders

Plato felt that those who most desire to rule are least suited to do so, because they invariably have ulterior motives. His solution was that leaders be conscripted into service the way soldiers are drafted into the military.

In a sense, the Biblical command for husbands to be leaders in their homes is exactly that—men being conscripted by God to serve their wives and children.

Unfortunately, most men are not natural leaders, nor do they naturally love their wives in the self-sacrificing, Christ-like way God commands. If these things came naturally, there'd be no need for the associated directives in Scripture. Commands in Scripture almost always run counter to our natural inclinations and underscore our need for the supernatural intervention of a loving Savior!

Do you long for your wife to shower you with respect and admiration? Do you wish she would follow your lead without arguing or questioning your every decision?

You will never get the results you are looking for by being harsh and demanding. Even if you were to gain her cooperation, it would be given begrudgingly. That isn't what godly servant-leadership looks like.

> "With great power comes great responsibility."[3]
>
> – Uncle Ben to Peter Parker

If you want your wife to follow your lead, then you must walk in a way that is worthy of respect. Lead in a way that inspires your family to follow.

Lead prayerfully. Lead gently. Guide them with humility, understanding, patience, faithfulness, temperance, and love.

As a husband, the responsibility falls to you for taking the lead in improving your marriage. Don't blame your wife for your own failures in this area. You must work to earn her trust and confidence.

Prove yourself to be a man of integrity, a person who thinks things through—not a man who is shortsighted or rash or vindictive.

It is a sobering proposition to be the spiritual head of one's home, to be held accountable before God for the spiritual health and welfare of one's family.

We should shoulder this responsibility with an attitude of meekness. Inwardly, our focus should not be, *"Alright!! I get to call the shots!"* Rather, we should be thinking, *"God has entrusted this responsibility to me, and I don't want to flub it up."*

Such a heavy responsibility calls for a posture of prayer. Pray that God will enable you to relate to your wife and children as a wise servant-leader should: Love them wholeheartedly. Love them sacrificially. Love them unconditionally. Love them extravagantly.

If you consistently shower your wife with that brand of love, chances are, it will eventually win her over and she'll happily follow you to the ends of the earth.

But what if it doesn't? What if she won't?

Then you've got to *keep on loving*. Love her, because God has commanded you to love her—not because of what you stand to gain from doing so. Love her and keep on loving her, because you want to be obedient to *Him.* He will receive the glory from your doing so. And that is the only success that will matter in the end.

> "The first responsibility of a leader is to define reality. The last is to say thank you. In between, the leader is a servant."
>
> – Max De Pree

Put It into Practice:

✎ Make a list of the things you desire in your spouse: consideration, compassion, a strong work ethic, patience, respect. Now, work on developing and modeling those same qualities yourself. Endeavor to lead your family by example.

✎ I've given the example of Christ washing his disciples feet and dying on their behalf, but there are plenty of examples of godly servant-leaders from modern times. I work in the healthcare industry and, although there are always exceptions, the vast majority of physicians and nurses put the patients' needs ahead of their own.

The book *Mountains Beyond Mountains* tells the story of Dr. Paul Farmer, a Harvard professor who works a few months each year in the United States so he can save up enough money to spend the rest of the year in Haiti, serving the poorest of the poor and sickest of the sick—a humbling and inspiring example to all of us.

Take time to read the biographies of Dr. Farmer and of other great servant-leaders in our not-too-distant past: George Washington, George Muller, Hudson Taylor, Amy Carmichael, and Gladys Aylward, to name just a few. Such accounts will inspire you to be a better leader yourself and to focus more consciously on addressing the needs of those you serve.

Intimacy
is a Two-Way
Street

Chapter 11

Unfortunately, men are notoriously selfish in the bedroom, yet are dumbfounded when their wives are less than enthusiastic in this arena. Make the intimacy part of your relationship as pleasurable for your wife as it is for you, and it will pay huge dividends.

How can you do this?

It may mean washing the dishes or helping with the kids, so that she has energy left at the end of the day for you. It may mean cuddling and candlelight, so that she can relax and let the worries on her mind drift away.

If you aren't sure where to begin, just ask her.

Then *listen* (refer to Chapter 1).

Don't just assume that your wife enjoys the same things you enjoy when it comes to intimacy, either. Remember to *value her individuality* (see Chapter 5).

Remember, too, that satisfaction for a woman takes TIME. It typically takes a woman longer to climax than a man. Ideally, a husband should view this delay as an opportunity to show his wife that sex means more to him than just personal gratification. He should take advantage of the opportunity to demonstrate the fact that *her* pleasure is as important to him as his own.

If your view of sex has never included the desire to gratify your wife in this way, then your view is too narrow and desperately needs to be broadened. As a husband, you have a moral obligation to think in such terms.

> "Among men, sex sometimes results in intimacy; among women, intimacy sometimes results in sex."
>
> – Barbara Cartland

The Jewish tradition of *onah* went to great lengths to ensure that a man satisfied the sexual needs of his wife, even to the point of specifying how often she could expect sex based on her husband's line of work. If her husband was a non-laborer—that is, if he worked with his brain rather than with his hands—she was entitled to nightly conjugal rights.

Moreover, a husband was not allowed to change from a job that entailed a high conjugal frequency to one associated with a lower conjugal frequency without first getting the approval of his wife to do so.

The Bible speaks to a husband's responsibility in this area, as well:

"The husband should fulfill his marital duty to his wife, and likewise the wife to her husband." (1 Corinthians 7:3, NASB)

If you think your wife needs to hear this verse more than you do, think again.

While the average man has a much stronger sex drive than the average woman, the average woman has a much shorter refractory period, making it possible for her to have multiple orgasms in a very short amount of time. If a man's body were capable of doing what hers can do, couples might *never* get out of bed.

> "The one thing we can never get enough of is love. And the one thing we never give enough is love."
>
> – Henry Miller

Unfortunately, if your wife is routinely unavailable or completely disinterested in sex, you may not have the opportunity to give her any orgasms at all. If the intimate part of your marriage is not all you expected it to be, you need to ask yourself why.

Commit the matter to prayer. Ask God to give you wisdom and discernment and a willingness to do what it takes to make the physical relationship in your marriage everything He intended it to be.

Every woman is different, but there are some underlying causes of sexual disinterest that are common to many of them. Prayerfully consider if any of these might be contributing to the problem in your marriage:

- **Lack of Time**

  Is your social life overscheduled? Has your wife stretched herself too thin?

  If you and she are always going in different directions so that you are seldom in the same place at the same time, it will be virtually impossible for you to ever connect.

  You may need to reassess your priorities. Cut back on outside commitments. Carve out some regular, predictable time together with your spouse and make sure nothing else bumps it off your schedule.

- **Lack of Energy**

  Maybe you're already spending plenty of time with your wife, but she's normally too tired to take full advantage of your time together.

  This is a natural consequence of living life at a breakneck pace, but it can happen even when you've been careful to preserve margin and keep whitespace on your calendar.

  Sometimes your wife may feel exhausted for reasons that may be difficult for you to see or understand. Pregnancy, breastfeeding, caring for young children or elderly parents—although these things don't necessarily take your wife away from home, they can so completely sap her energy stores that she has little or nothing left over at the end of the day to give to you.

If this is the case, you may need to set aside time earlier in the day for physical intimacy, before her reserves are depleted. Pitch in with necessary chores and take what you can off her plate. If you can afford to do so, hire help with housecleaning or take her out to dinner. If your wife is on the brink of exhaustion, she will appreciate all the help she can get.

• Lack of Confidence

Sometimes when a wife is self-conscious about her appearance, it will make her avoid sex. Do your best to build her up in this area. She needs to know that you still find her attractive.

Be tender and encouraging and generous with your compliments. Never tease your wife in any way that would make her feel ashamed of her body. Make her feel safe sharing herself with you by admiring her openly and often.

• Lack of Understanding

I think many women just don't understand how vitally important physical intimacy is to the majority of husbands. If your wife can go for days or weeks without thinking about sex, she may wonder why you can't do the same. Even if she really enjoys sex, she may not desire it as often as you do.

If there is a wide discrepancy between your individual drives, discuss the matter with your wife in a calm, non-accusatory way.

Ask her what you can do to make sex as pleasurable an experience for her as it is for you. Describe how prioritizing sex would not only draw you closer together and strengthen your marriage, but it would provide each of you with a wide variety of physical, mental and emotional benefits, as well.[1]

- **Lack of Trust**

  Understand that if you've done anything during the course of your marriage to violate your wife's trust, it can have long lasting repercussions.

  If you have been guilty of being unfaithful to your wife—either in thought or deed—I urge you to repent, seek forgiveness from both God and your spouse, and completely forsake your sin in the future. The success of your marriage depends on it.

  You do not have to have sex outside of marriage to be guilty of adultery. Jesus said, *"Anyone who looks at a woman lustfully has already committed adultery with her in his heart."* (Matthew 5:28, NIV)

Clearly, Christ's words would also preclude any use of pornography. Pornography is all about looking at women with lustful intent, and few things will destroy trust, undermine unity, and derail intimacy in a marriage faster than porn.

Many men attempt to justify their porn use by pointing fingers at non-responsive wives. And the wives point right back at their porn-addicted husbands to explain their lack of interest.

Porn use preys on your wife's insecurities about her own body and about her ability to attract and keep your attention. It causes her to question whether she has ever satisfied you sexually in the past or has any hope of doing so in the future.

> "Real connection and intimacy is like a meal, not a sugar fix."
>
> – Kristin Armstrong

The more you turn to porn for sexual release, the more justified your wife will feel in shutting you out.

And the more she shuts you out, the more desperately you will consume the porn. It is a vicious cycle in which everyone loses, and it will gut your marriage unless you break the cycle—and quickly.

You must give up the porn. Cold turkey. Turn your back on it completely.

You cannot make this step contingent upon your wife's meeting your needs for sexual intimacy. Assume that isn't going to happen for a long time, if ever. Your addiction has undoubtedly hurt her, and it will take time to reestablish her trust in you.

That doesn't change what you have to do. You must commit to living a life of purity both in thought and deed. You must determine to walk in integrity, regardless of your wife's response. This is what God's Word requires of you.

In the meantime, pray that God would meet your need for physical intimacy *through your wife*. Pray that He would heal the hurt, restore the trust, and enable you to love her in an unselfish, sacrificial way.

> "You can't make your own obedience to Scripture contingent on somebody else's performance."
>
> – Jennifer Flanders

Then be patient while He works on her heart.

There will likely be some lag time between your forsaking porn and your wife's realization that you've given it up for good. Don't let that deter you.

The forced sexual fast you endure in the interim will act like a sensory deprivation booth, priming you to give and take pleasure in the real thing like never before.

By using porn, you've been subsisting on a diet of junk food in its foulest form. You've become so stuffed with empty calories that your appetite for good, wholesome, nutritious food has been seriously compromised, if not utterly destroyed.

Doing without any food at all will help you to more fully enjoy and appreciate the good stuff when it is later presented.

Married, monogamous sex is a marvelous, miraculous thing. Just remember that it's not what you *get*, but what you *give*, that's important.

Make it your goal to make it good for her, and you'll feel your own pleasure rocket to new heights.

Put It into Practice:

✍ If you haven't already done so, invest in a good, child-proof lock for your master bedroom door. Especially if you have children, intimacy will happen more easily when you don't have to worry about little ones walking in on you when you're in the middle of the act.

✍ Run your wife some water and let her soak in a warm bath before bedtime. If the tub is big enough for two, join her there, or take a hot shower together. There is something about being fresh, clean, and relaxed that makes sex even more appealing.

✍ If you have never taken time to find out what pleases your wife in the area of sex, set aside time to do so without delay. If possible, schedule a weekend away. Remember that for a woman, sex encompasses far more than just the physical act.

✍ If your wife smokes, drinks, takes certain forms of medication, or if she is post-menopausal, it may adversely affect her ability to climax. If you suspect such a factor may be at play in your relationship, urge her to discuss the matter with her doctor.

✍ Be patient. It takes most women significantly longer to orgasm than it does men. Don't make your wife feel pressured "to perform." Instead, make every effort to learn how and where she would like to be touched to bring maximum pleasure to her—even if that just means rubbing her back or cuddling for a little longer than usual.

Give Her
Time to
Herself

Chapter 12

Everyone needs an occasional break to rest and recharge. The gospels tell us that even Jesus often withdrew to lonely places to pray.[1]

A little time to rest and reflect is especially important for a woman who is at home all day with young children. Yet it is very easy to neglect this legitimate need unless you regularly and intentionally schedule time for it.

"Time to herself" will mean different things to different women. Perhaps your wife craves female fellowship and will choose to use this time to connect with friends over coffee. Maybe she dreams of having enough time to herself to have her hair done or get a manicure—or maybe just take a bath or a nap without interruption.

Perhaps your wife simply longs for a little peace and quiet—the opportunity to hear herself think. This is the case for my wife, who is perfectly content with a little alone time in the wee hours of the morning while the rest of the family sleeps. A morning person through and through, she enjoys having those solitary hours to write or to work on other projects undisturbed.

Whatever "time to herself" means to your wife, find out and make provision for it on a regular basis.

Women are communicators at heart; so make sure she has a regular outlet for adult conversation, both by taking time to engage her in conversation yourself and by being supportive of her friendships with other women.

> "You
> only grow
> when you're
> alone."
>
> – Paul Newman

Granted, this seems more vitally important to some women than others.

If female friendship appears to be a deep need for your wife, facilitate it as well as you can. Encourage her to attend a MOPS (Mothers of Preschoolers) group or a weekly women's Bible study (such as Bible Study Fellowship) or a homeschool co-op.

Sunday fellowship dinners served this purpose for many of the women in our home church, including my wife. For nearly a decade, we toted our crockpot to church with us every week. Then—once the sermon was over and the last hymn had been sung—our entire congregation would sit down and eat a potluck lunch together. The food merely nourished our bodies; the fellowship nourished our souls.

If your wife is one who doesn't crave conversation as much as she longs to get a leg up on her lengthy to-do list, consider pitching in to help her get ahead. Or maybe take little ones to run errands so she can get some work done without them underfoot.

If the children are old enough, train them to help, as well, so your wife won't feel like she has to spend all her time cleaning up after the rest of the family. In fact, if your wife is routinely working while the rest of you are playing, something is probably amiss.

She may need you to step in and help delegate some chores. Don't hesitate to do this if the situation calls for it.

She has hopes and dreams and hobbies she'd like to pursue, just like the rest of the family, and she'll appreciate your help in making time for that to happen.

Put It into Practice:

✍ Talk to your wife about taking some time for herself. Is that something she desires? How can you help her get it?

✍ When dinner is over, don't leave your wife to do the dishes while you prop up your feet in front of the television. Pitch in to help, and teach your children to do the same. You'll knock out the chores in short order, then you can all relax and do something fun together.

✍ Get in the habit of taking a child or two along with you whenever you run errands. If your wife is at home with little ones all day, she'll appreciate even this short break.

✍ Alternatively, if your kids are older, leave them at home (with or without assigned chores to accomplish while your gone) and take your wife along to run the errands. Even "grocery store dates" can provide a much-needed break from the routine and give the two of you an opportunity to visit and enjoy one another's company.

Set Aside
Couple Time

Chapter 13

You dated your wife before you married and had a wonderful time doing so. That fact shouldn't end, just because you've tied the knot. Why not do all you can to keep this good thing going?

Dating doesn't need to be fancy or formal. It doesn't have to cost a lot of money. It doesn't necessarily mean you even have to leave home—although a little variety can be fun, too.

Whatever gets the two of you alone for some quality time on a regular basis should be considered a date. This can be a daily thing, a weekly thing, an annual thing or (preferably) a combination thereof.

While my wife and I will occasionally go out to eat (without the kids), take in a movie, or attend some banquet, for as long as we can remember, our standing "date" has been every evening after dinner and family time. Our children are sent to their rooms to read quietly in bed, while the two of us retire to ours to soak in the tub, talk about the day, and spend a little alone time together.

> "Most men think the mission ends after they marry the woman they love, that the most exciting and rewarding work is over... The reality is that the mission has only just begun."
>
> - Justin Buzzard

We enjoy connecting this way each day, and doing so consistently has been a large part of what has kept our love for one another fresh and our marriage strong for so many years now.

One writer I respect suggests scheduling regular planning meetings with your spouse to discuss goals and projects for the coming week, month, quarter or year. My wife and I have always done this informally, but as our children have gotten older and our lives become more complex, we've had to be more intentional about setting aside time for these vision-casting discussions.

Certainly, these planning meetings count as spending time together, but not all dates need to be such pre-scheduled, formal affairs. Running a few errands together, taking a stroll around the block, or spending a few minutes holding hands on the porch swing qualifies as couple time, too.

Here are a few more ideas to help you out of the dinner-and-a-movie mentality. Pick and choose the ones that appeal to you:

- Go out for ice cream.
- Visit a local museum.
- Attend a concert—or a free dress rehearsal.
- Go to a library or bookstore and browse.
- Pack a picnic and eat outdoors.
- Play Scrabble or some other board game.
- Ride bikes together.
- Walk around the block.
- Go to the zoo (or visit a pet store).
- Cheer on the high school football team.
- Go stargazing. Bring a quilt if it's chilly.
- Swim—and take turns jumping off the board.
- Play Putt-Putt golf.
- Check out nearby historical markers.
- Shop garage sales.
- Go for a jog. Maybe even train for a race.
- Take dancing lessons.
- Enroll in continuing education classes.
- Run errands together.
- Go antiquing.
- Graze on free samples from Sam's.
- Grab a cup of coffee.
- Fly a kite.
- Take a hike.
- Go to a park.

25 Ways to Show Love to Your Wife

- Go parking—and make out in the back seat.
- Attend a school musical or play.
- Build a fire and roast marshmallows.
- Go bowling.
- Plant some flowers.
- Go to the beach and build sandcastles.
- Go for a drive (or test drive a new car).
- Do chores together.
- Clean out the garage.
- Pop popcorn and watch a video.
- Rake leaves (then roll in them, too).
- Skate at the nearest roller rink.
- Go grocery shopping as a couple.
- Cook together.
- Eat by candlelight.
- Pitch a tent and sleep out in the backyard.
- Work a jigsaw puzzle.
- Play Ping-Pong at the community center.
- Tour model homes together.
- Look at scrapbooks or old photo albums.
- Soak in a hot bath or take a shower together.
- Go to bed early (but not straight to sleep).
- Read aloud to one another (then discuss what you've read).

I could go on and on. The options are endless.

The important thing is not so much *what* you do, but that you do it *together*. So find something you both enjoy and set aside some time to regularly spend as a couple—just the two of you.

Put It into Practice:

✍ Grab your wife and your calendar and sit down together to carve out some alone time over the next few weeks or months. Put it on the schedule, and make every effort to keep that commitment.

✍ Review the list of ideas on pp. 73-74. Mark the ones that appeal most to you and have your wife do the same, then work off that short list next time you need inspiration on date night.

✍ Don't feel like dates have to take you away from home. Although my wife and I enjoy going out occasionally, we both agree our most meaningful "couple time" takes place within the four walls of our own house.

✍ For a fun list of activities specific to your area, check the event calendar in your local paper. You'll find information about all sorts of things you and your wife can enjoy—upcoming festivals, art shows, church bazaars, and parks programs—much of it for free. Many cities sponsor free fine arts performances such as Shakespeare in the Park or Symphony under the Stars. You'll also find information in the same section of the paper on local charity runs—5K, 10K, half or full marathons. Why not pick one and start training?

Be Careful
with Female
Friendship

Chapter 14

We all have friends and colleagues of the opposite sex, and it is important that we learn to interact with them in a healthy way—especially once we marry.

If you're very newly wed, then you have likely spent a good portion of your life trying to "find" the right girl to marry. Now that you've found her, you must get out of "search" mode. The charm and flirtatiousness that served you so well when you were single is now a liability, not an asset.

If you have been married awhile, then you've probably already figured out a lot of the things I'm about to discuss. Nonetheless, the occasional reminder can be helpful, since many of us tend to forget or neglect the basics as the years go by.

To begin, let me state that being married doesn't make you a monk. You don't get to live in a monastery somewhere, shielded from any association with females outside your family.

> "It is not someone else's responsibility to honor my marriage. It's my responsibility."
>
> - David Duchovny

You still have to live in the real world, work a job, and interact with living, breathing human beings, roughly half of which are women.

For this reason, a few basic rules of engagement are in order. Four basic principles should guide a husband's interaction with women other than his wife:

First, you must *protect your reputation.* As a married person, this becomes dramatically more important since the stakes are so much higher.

Second, you must *protect your heart*. Affairs don't happen in a vacuum, they develop over time. Don't let them.

Third, you must *be considerate of your wife's feelings.* Sounds simple, but it can be more complicated than it seems. How men view certain words or actions and how their wives view them can vary significantly. Beware the landmines!

And last, *you must be considerate of your female friend's significant other*. It doesn't take much to instigate jealousy or even anger in their partner if you aren't careful.

Protect Your Reputation

Reputations, as they say, take a lifetime to build but only an instant to destroy. This is even truer in the modern era where people thirst for negative news and are quick to believe the worst. Superimpose the lightening speed of modern communications, and you have a recipe for disaster.

Don't let it happen to you. Or, as author Jon Acuff's wife advises him, "Don't go viral for the wrong reasons!"

There are several simple ways to avoid this problem.

First, do not be alone with any woman who is not your wife.

Does that sound a little harsh? Old fashioned, perhaps? Maybe even puritanical?

> "It takes a lifetime to build a good reputation, but you can lose it in a minute."
>
> - Will Rogers

It is sound advice, nonetheless, and may someday save your reputation and very likely your marriage if only you will follow it. Why risk ever becoming embroiled in a "he said/she said" misunderstanding when it can so easily be avoided?

Life is too full of traps and temptations as it is, why set snares for your own feet unnecessarily? Once there is an asterisk by your reputation, it never goes away.

The second principle is a corollary to the first: Don't spend an excessive amount of time with a woman who is not your wife, even in public.

When your co-workers or friends notice the two of you together all the time, either laughing and joking, or engaged in deep, serious conversation, they begin to wonder *why?* Their imaginations will quickly answer that question for them, regardless of how innocent your relationship may be. It's no longer a "he said/she said" situation, but quickly becomes a matter of what "they said" behind your back.

Steer clear of clandestine rendezvous with friends or acquaintances of the opposite gender. Always be honest and forthcoming with your wife concerning what you do when you're apart from her, and with whom. Keeping secrets spells trouble no matter how you slice it.

> "Once you've said 'I do,' your relationship with your spouse must now take priority over every other relationship, and it must be protected against any threat."
>
> - Dr. Debbie Cherry

Furthermore, some subjects should be off limits for discussion between you and someone of the opposite sex.

Bawdy humor is an obvious example. Another is the discussion of marital discord, either yours or hers. Such discussion, if necessary, should always be redirected to a trusted friend or counselor of the same sex. Expressing dissatisfaction with a spouse very commonly becomes a pretext to finding solace in someone else's arms. Don't take that chance.

I don't mean to imply you cannot have female friends, nor am I advocating making such relationships weird and awkward. I've known people who refuse to even look members of the opposite sex in the eye, lest they come across as being too familiar. In my opinion, they've let the pendulum swing too far in the other direction, making it hard to have even the simplest of exchanges.

Interacting with other women is both possible and necessary, but you must be careful how and where you invest the bulk of your time and energy. It's more a question of degree—if your dearest and best friend is a woman who isn't your wife, then it's clearly time to reassess.

> "Happy is the man who finds a true friend, and far happier is he who finds that true friend in his wife."
>
> - Franz Schubert

Guard Your Heart

Tread cautiously when relating to female friends and acquaintances. Not all affairs are physical ones. Honoring your marriage vows means remaining faithful in thought and word, as well as in deed.

It's understandable that we would become close with our coworkers. After all, we spend forty hours or more together every week. In some cases, this may mean we actually spend more waking hours together with them than we do with our spouses.

Some of those coworkers may be single. Some may be happily married. Some unhappily married.

Many of them will be smart, attractive, kind, filled with many admirable qualities that your spouse may or may not share. But at the end of the day, no matter how wonderful your female colleagues may be, none of those women are your wife, nor should they be treated as such.

Your wife is the only woman with whom you should cultivate physical, spiritual, and emotional intimacy. She's the one you should live with, confide in, depend on, and bare your soul to.

The harsh reality is that the woman at work or the gym who seems to *get you* only does so because she doesn't have to *live with you.* She's only observed the "fitness" version of you or the "dressed up and working hard" version of you.

She has never seen the "flatulent, half-dressed, hair a mess, haven't bathed in two days, sports-watching, short-tempered, forgot to pick up the milk, bring in the mail, or pay the bills on time" version of you.

> "It's okay and even valuable to have opposite-sex friends. Yet... it's both unwise and dangerous to spend one-on-one time with them after you're married."
>
> - Gary Oliver

And that version of you isn't nearly so attractive.

Your wife sees and knows all of you, not just the cherry-picked, carefully polished facets of your personality. She knows you as a real and complete person, not some smoke and mirrors illusion.

That other woman doesn't.

In similar fashion, the notion that you've found a "soul mate" other than your wife is pure fantasy.

That woman at work or the gym only seems amazing because you don't have to live with her annoying idiosyncrasies, her inexplicable mood swings, her spitefulness when upset, or any of a myriad other things that can so quickly extinguish the hottest flames of passion.

> "Be careful how and where you invest the bulk of your time and energy."
>
> - Doug Flanders

If talent and beauty were the only ingredients necessary for a long, happy, successful marriage, then Hollywood stars would never get divorced.

Men who stray eventually come to realize the grass on the other side of the fence isn't as green as they initially thought. Unfortunately, that realization often comes after it's too late.

Don't destroy the hope you have for happiness in your present marriage by seeking happiness elsewhere. All meaningful, lasting relationships take work. They demand intentionality.

To know and be known requires an investment of time and energy.

Invest in your wife.

Consider Your Wife's Feelings

The third rule is to be considerate of your wife's feelings in how you relate to other women.

Such consideration comes in two varieties: *how you interact with other women* and *how you speak about other women*. The short version is: don't be too positive or negative in either situation. Relative neutrality is key.

> "Never make your spouse feel that she isn't the most important relationship to you."
>
> - Sharon Rivkin

Let's start with how you interact with other women. When your wife is present, assume her radar is up. You shouldn't eyeball the gorgeous woman in the skimpy outfit who just walked into the room, even in your wife's absence, but when your spouse is sitting right beside you, you certainly better refrain from gawking.

The same goes for such women in the movies or on television. Your wife needs your assurance that you have eyes only for her.

Likewise, don't get enmeshed in a two-hour conversation off in the corner at a party with that cute new girl from work, as steam slowly pours from your spouse's ears. And, most importantly of all, *never ever ever flirt with anybody but your wife!*

Of course, you can be kind and hospitable without being flirtatious, and I recommend you do so, especially when relating to your wife's friends. Her friends are constantly judging you and providing feedback, solicited or otherwise, and it would serve you well to be in their good graces.

This really isn't that hard. Common courtesy and small talk can go a long way. While you don't want your wife's girlfriends to think you're coming on to them, neither do you want them to think you are rude. Learn to walk the line. Be friendly, not flirty.

But how you behave *toward other women* is only half the equation, and the more straightforward half, at that. The really tricky part hinges on how you speak *about other women.*

You obviously can't be too complimentary—especially about looks. However, if you are too dismissive of unusual beauty or talent, your wife will become suspicious and question your judgment, including your judgment of her.

A good rule of thumb is to compliment talent without gushing, but say nothing regarding looks, unless she specifically asks.

> "Never ever *ever* flirt with anybody but your wife."
>
> - Doug Flanders

If she does ask, be careful—she is testing you. The correct answer is to mildly acknowledge beauty, so as not to appear dense, but to include a modifying caveat, so as to reaffirm your loyalty.

You might answer, for example, "Yes, she is tall and thin, but it makes her seem frail. I have always preferred a more athletic build, like yours. It just seems healthier and more robust."

Again, you must also be cautious with the flip side. You should not be overly critical of other women, especially of their appearance. The most serious and stoic of women are highly self-conscious about their looks. In their minds, criticism of one woman translates into criticism of all women.

This is especially true regarding weight. If you casually mention some other woman has gained weight, your wife will immediately assume that you are insinuating she, herself, has packed on a few too many pounds, as well. Just don't do it. That discussion is a tar baby made with extra sticky tar.

Be Considerate of Significant Others

All humans are territorial, and men particularly so. You don't want the spouse/fiancé/boyfriend of your female friend or co-worker to view you as a threat or a competitor. You should be neither, and your behavior should reflect that fact.

A moment of cuteness or flirtatiousness on your end can translate into a lot of heartache and misery on hers. Don't do that to a friend.

Just as you should avoid flirting with other women, you should also take appropriate measures to keep them from flirting with you. Neither engage in it yourself nor encourage it from them.

That's why it's so important—not only for your own marriage, but also for others'—that clear boundaries are set. Rarely if ever do these boundaries have to be explicitly stated. Usually just talking about your children and your spouse in glowing terms (see chapter 3) early on and repeatedly thereafter will clarify the situation for everyone involved without things becoming unnecessarily uncomfortable or awkward.

Chapter 14 – Be Careful with Female Friendship

The same principle holds true in social settings—especially whenever alcohol is served. I remember attending an out-of-town, obligatory social event several years ago at which a woman who'd obviously had too much to drink came over to me, draped her arms around my neck, and asked what I'd be doing later that night.

When I politely explained that I would be talking on the phone to my lovely wife and our eight kids, she dropped her arms in stunned surprise and quickly moved on in search of a more receptive companion.

A couple months later, the woman was divorced. She evidently found somebody who shared her lack of concern for maintaining proper boundaries or showing appropriate consideration of her spouse.

If you want your marriage to last and your wife to feel loved, you'll have to do better than that.

Put It into Practice:

✍ If you've been guilty of investing yourself in a relationship with a woman who is not your wife, find a way to redirect those funds of time and emotion back towards the one you married. Force yourself to exercise marriage-building habits.

✍ Make your wife your exercise partner. If she hates the gym, but likes walking the dog, then learn to enjoy a nice stroll around the neighborhood.

✍ If you've grown fond of brainstorming over lunch with a female co-worker, try calling your wife and chatting with her instead.

✍ If there has been any friction in the past between you and your wife caused by opposite-sex relationships, discuss the matter and agree upon some guidelines that will govern how you both approach such friendships in the future.

Use Good
Hygiene

Chapter 15

It is amazing how meticulous guys can be prior
to marriage. When they are trying to impress the girls,
they take great care with their appearance. But for many
of us, once we walk down the aisle, all bets are off.

It's time to bring back those glory days. Clean up
a little. It won't kill you—I promise.

You like for your wife to look fresh, don't you?
It makes you happy when she wears clean, pretty clothes
and takes time to wash and style her hair.

So why not show her the same courtesy?

I don't know whether cleanliness is really next to
godliness, but it sure makes living with a person more
pleasant when you don't have to contend with bad breath

or body odor—and I'm betting your wife would agree with that statement.

I read an article recently on the nine most unkempt stars in Hollywood—actors and actresses who, despite amazing success at the box office, still haven't mastered the most basic habits of daily hygiene, such as bathing, using deodorant, or washing their hair with any sense of regularity.[1]

> "Ya know what I do almost every day? I wash. Personal hygiene is part of the package with me."
>
> - Jim Carrey

Consequently, their co-workers often gossip behind their backs (or to the press) about how bad these celebrities smell and what a trial it is to work with them.

Steve Jobs shared their aversion to good hygiene and was purportedly assigned to the night shift at Atari because of his stench.[2]

Don't make your wife wish she could similarly isolate you. Exercise good, basic hygiene. Do it for your own health, as well as for the benefit of everyone who must live or work in close contact with you.

These basics include:

- Showering or bathing daily—or multiple times a day if you're especially sweaty from work or exercise
- Using deodorant or antiperspirant (if you slather your armpits with Purell® once a week before applying deodorant, you'll kill

most of the odor-causing bacteria that reside there)

- Brushing your teeth regularly (flossing and using mouthwash or whitening strips is a bonus)
- Shaving and/or keeping your facial hair neatly trimmed
- Keeping your hair clean and neatly cut (use anti-dandruff shampoo as needed)
- Dressing in clean, fresh-smelling clothes with no rips or stains
- Washing your hands frequently, especially before meals and after using the restroom
- Keeping your nails clean and trimmed
- Covering your nose and mouth when you have to cough or sneeze (instead of coughing into your hand, which can itself spread germs, try coughing into the crook of your arm or down the collar of your shirt, instead)

"Take care of your body. It's the only place you have to live."

- Jim Rohn

As you can see, this is all pretty basic stuff. It's the kind of stuff those around you likely take for granted—until you start to let it slide.

So don't.

Stay on top of it, and your wife will be proud to be seen with you in public.

Put It into Practice:

✍ Yes, you should bathe every day, but it doesn't have to be a solo activity. Invite your wife to join you in the shower or tub. The two of you can get squeaky clean together.

✍ Take your wife's preferences into consideration next time you visit the barbershop. Does she like the feel of a stubby crew cut, or would she prefer you leave a few curls behind your ears? As much as possible, do your best to accommodate her.

✍ The same goes for facial hair: Some women love thick beards or stylish soul patches. My wife tells me my whiskers scratch when I kiss her, so I normally keep clean-shaven for her sake.

✍ I understand the need for wearing grubby clothes to do messy jobs like painting or yard work, but you probably don't need a whole closet full of them. Save a shirt or two that you won't mind getting ruined, but donate or recycle the rest of those stained and holey T's and invest in some clothes that make you look more presentable, even when you're going casual.

Limit the
Gross Stuff

Chapter 16

Women seldom find burping, farting, or mooning nearly as hilarious as guys do, and—chances are—your wife is no exception. If you love her and have not already done so, you must learn to limit the gross stuff.

Cut out the coarse jokes, the booger picking, the potty humor, the burp talking, the forced flatulence, and all the other stuff you've been laughing at since junior high and show a little courtesy—at least for as long as she's in the room or within earshot.

This doesn't mean you won't still need to pass gas or clean your nose from time to time; it only means you won't make an exhibition of doing so in front of your wife.

Not only will your wife appreciate this newfound consideration, but your children will benefit, as well, because they'll have fewer bad habits to emulate.

Children have always been keener on mimicking behavior than on following instructions. If you consistently model good manners at home, you'll have less cause for humiliation when your kids act out or repeat in public the things they've seen you do or say in private.

> "The hardest job kids face today is learning good manners without seeing any."
>
> - Fred Astaire

Of course, it isn't enough to just cut out the bad stuff. Doing *that* will merely create a vacuum, until something equally bad or worse replaces the ousted behaviors.[1]

Instead, we must work to *exchange* undesirable habits for exemplary ones. Good manners and kindness, as the saying goes, are always in fashion, so why not start there?

Saying "please," "thank you," "excuse me," and "you're welcome," holding doors open for your wife, carrying heavy loads for her, helping her with her coat, being protective in general—these gestures were once considered *common courtesies*, but they aren't so common anymore.

And what a tangible way to demonstrate love for your wife and set an example for others to follow! Go a step further and teach your sons to show such courtesies to their mother. By the time they marry, then, it should be second nature, and their wives will thank you for training them so well.

Militant feminists would have us to believe it is sexist to show such courtesies to women. That is just a bunch of bunk.

> "You can get through life with bad manners, but it's easier with good manners."
>
> - Lillian Gish

I know your wife is probably very capable of opening her own doors and carrying her own packages.

Mine is, too.

But just because they *can* do such things doesn't mean they *should*. Or that we should let them.

The good manners you demonstrate toward your spouse reflect honor and consideration for her, but they also reflect a healthy respect for yourself.

Men are not animals, despite some angry claims to the contrary. By the empowering grace of God, and when given the opportunity to demonstrate such virtues, men can be extraordinarily kind and noble and self-sacrificing.

Marriage is exactly the opportunity we need, as the vast majority of women enjoy being treated with such gentle compassion. In all likelihood, your wife still wants to envision you as her knight in shining armor.

So act the part.

Put It into Practice:

✍ 1 Peter 3:8 tells us, *"Be like-minded, be sympathetic, love one another, be compassionate and humble."* The King James Version translates that last part, *"Be courteous."* This isn't a suggestion; it's a command. Are you making a sincere effort to follow it in the way you relate to your wife?

✍ Is it time for your manners to get a makeover? Think back to when you first met your wife. Were there small kindnesses and courtesies you showed her then that you've let slip since? Maybe it's time to resurrect them.

✍ Being courteous is as much about the things you don't do as the things you do. Ephesians 5:4 lists several bad habits that need to be banned: *"And there must be no filthiness and silly talk, or coarse jesting, which are not fitting, but rather giving of thanks."* Examine yourself. Do you use language or tell jokes when you're around the guys that you'd be ashamed to let slip when you're with your wife? Then maybe you shouldn't be talking like that *at all.*

✍ Clean up your act. Doing so is a sure way to make your wife feel cherished.

Be
Patient

Chapter 17

Praying for patience is a little like asking some one to tape a "Kick Me" sign on your back. There's no easy way to learn it, except to endure countless events that drive you crazy.

Opportunities to practice patience fall into two broad categories, and I'd be hard-pressed to say which is most important.

The first category is acute circumstances that call for patience: You're stuck in traffic. You're waiting for a reply to an important text or phone call. Somebody is doing something that drives you absolutely nuts.

What's your instinctive response? If it involves angry words, exasperated sighs, long-winded lectures, or skyrocketing blood pressures, then it's time to change your habits. Take a deep breath and focus on being kind, remaining calm, and not overreacting.

Of course, exercising patience does not mean you don't deal with the problems that arise; it only dictates that you deal with them in a logical, loving way, rather than in a cycle of rage and regret. Scripture implores us to *"admonish the unruly, encourage the fainthearted, help the weak, be patient with everyone."* (1 Thessalonians 5:13-14, NASB)

The second (and more difficult) category of patience-trying opportunities involves chronic or long-term problems. These would include major life changes: You go bankrupt. You lose a loved one. You're diagnosed with an incurable, debilitating illness.

But it can also include comparatively minor stuff: Nobody is actively getting on your nerves in a dramatic sort of way, but nonetheless, you must still draw deeply and repeatedly from your reserves of patience as they slowly mature over time.

> "Patience is not the ability to wait. Waiting is a fact of life. Patience is the ability to keep a good attitude while waiting."
>
> - Joyce Meyers

Your spouse, your children, your friends—and, indeed, you yourself—are all works in progress. We emerge from the womb knowing nothing, and go to our graves knowing little more. In every area of life, we are in a continual process of acquiring knowledge and experience, of progressing from nothing to little of nothing.

By definition, each person we know is either behind us, ahead of us, or right there beside us on this continuum of growth. If ahead, we call them a teacher. Behind us, we call them a student. With us, we call them a companion.

When we find ourselves in the role of teacher, we must be patient with our students. When we find ourselves in the role of students, we must often be patient with ourselves. And always, we should be a comfort to our companions.

> "Without patience, we will learn less in life. We will see less. We will feel less. We will hear less. Ironically, *rush* and *more* usually mean *less.*"
>
> - Mother Teresa

You will find that your wife is a combination of all three of these roles. She will be ahead of you in some areas and behind in others: Sometimes, your teacher. Sometimes, your student. Always, your companion.

God designed each of you to complement the other. Accordingly, you both have different strengths and different weaknesses.

When we fall short in the area of acute patience —snapping at people because they didn't do things precisely the way we like them—the underlying issue is usually one of pride. It is a forgetfulness of where we once were on the learning continuum or an exaggeration of where we are now on that same continuum.

Patience recognizes that proficiency grows over time—we have not always been as skilled as we are now. Patience is also mindful of the fact that, even at our present skill-level, we can still make mistakes.

> "Have courage
> for the great sorrows
> of life and patience
> for the small ones;
> and when
> you have laboriously
> accomplished
> your daily task,
> go to sleep in peace.
> God is awake."
>
> - Victor Hugo

When we fail in the area of long-term patience, it is often due to a lack of vision. We fail to see what the other person could become; we see them only as they are now.

Goethe once said, "If you treat an individual as he is, he will remain how he is. But if you treat him as if he were what he ought to be and could be, he will become what he ought to be and could be."

This goes for your wife, too. God has charged you to live with her in an understanding way, to treat her with patience and gentleness, as a weaker vessel.[1] So bear with her. Don't expect perfection from her. Be patient with her. Love her.

This is what the Word of God requires of us, not only in the way we relate to our wives, but to our children and to the other people He places in our path, as well:

Chapter 17 – Be Patient

*So, as those who have been chosen of God, holy and beloved, **put on a heart of compassion, kindness, humility, gentleness and patience; bearing with one another, and forgiving each other**, whoever has a complaint against anyone; just as the Lord forgave you, so also should you. Beyond all these things **put on love**, which is the perfect bond of unity. **Let the peace of Christ rule in your hearts**, to which indeed you were called in one body; and **be thankful**.*

*- Colossians 3:12-15, NASB **(emphasis added)***

The peace of Christ, ruling in your heart. Is that what your wife and children witness when you are irritated? Is it what your friends and family see when you face frustration? When somebody's pushing your buttons, do you respond with humility, kindness, and gentleness?

As a Christian, that is what we are called to do. It's a tall order, and I'll be the first to admit that I often fail the test.

I've never cheated on my wife or beaten her or abandoned her, and in light of that stellar track record, it's tempting to excuse the fact that I sometimes lose patience or say things I shouldn't say using tones I shouldn't use. But God has

> "Face your deficiencies and acknowledge them; but do not let them master you. Let them teach you patience, sweetness, insight."
>
> - Helen Keller

been convicting me lately that, in His eyes, there are no "small" sins. My moments of impatience toward my wife are grievous to Him, and they should be grievous to me—just as yours should be to you.

God isn't interested in excuses or explanations or justifications for *why* we let our patience lapse. Nor is He impressed by half-hearted apologies or requests for forgiveness that aren't accompanied by genuine repentance.

> "My impatience is grievous to God— and should be grievous to me."
>
> - Doug Flanders

It isn't enough to admit impatience is sin if we then persist in our bad habits.

God is calling us to turn away from our sin. To give up our irritated, impatient, prideful ways and allow Him to remake us in the image of Christ. Are you willing to let Him do that?

He wants to develop in us the fruit of the Spirit, among which patience is high on the list:

> *"But the fruit of the Spirit is love, joy, peace, patience, kindness, goodness, faithfulness, gentleness, self-control; against such things there is no law."*
>
> - Galatians 5:22-23 (NASB)

Patience is also a defining characteristic of love, as we see in 1 Corinthians 13:

> *"Love is patient, love is kind... is not provoked, does not take into account a wrong suffered...*

bears all things, believes all things, hopes all things, endures all things."

You want to show your wife how much you love her? Start by showing patience, and she's sure to get the message.

Put It into Practice:

✍ Be patient, *be patient,* be *patient* with your wife! In whatever way this applies to you, apply it. Use the times you are tempted to respond impatiently as reminders that you still need more practice. As with body building and endurance training, the more you exercise your patience, the stronger it will become. So change your responses accordingly, until patience becomes a habit.

✍ Hasty words and irritated tones are not the only ways to communicate impatience. You can broadcast the same thing by tapping your foot, rolling your eyes, clicking your tongue, drumming your fingers, or heaving an exasperated sigh. So let Christ calm your spirit, then make sure your body language reflects the change.

✍ In what areas are you more knowledgeable than your wife? Are you a patient teacher? In what areas is your wife more knowledgeable than you? How can you be a better student and learn from her?

Cherish
Her
Children

Chapter 18

People who don't have children will sometimes tell people who do have children, "I know exactly what it's like raising kids—I have a dog." At which point, those of us who do have children want to scream, "It's not the same thing! NOT. EVEN. CLOSE."

But we don't scream this, for two reasons: One, we want to keep our friends. And two, we felt the same way before we had kids ourselves.

Admit it. Didn't you ever see a child misbehave in some spectacular way and think, "My kids will *never* do that"—despite the fact you didn't even have kids at the time? It's easy to be a parenting expert *before* you're a parent (and it's inevitably necessary to eat your words after)!

Of course, our dog-loving friends aren't making that lame comparison to be mean. They're 100% sincere and really believe what they're saying is true. No doubt, they love their pets very dearly, yet the bond between parent and child is something that cannot be fully understood until you have a child of your own.

In like manner, I do not feel that men can truly, completely understand the bond that a mother has with a child she has carried within her womb for nine months and nursed at her breast a year or two beyond that. As much as we fathers love our children, our wives love them in a different and special way, possibly even more.

> "It is easier for a father to have children than for children to have a real father."
>
> - Pope John XXIII

The good news is, this allows fathers to dish out "tough love" when necessary—although it's important to do so cautiously. Unnecessary harshness toward your children will not only harm your relationship with them, but will also damage your relationship with your spouse (a concept that is amplified even further when you're dealing with stepchildren).

But the converse is also true. Kindness towards them counts as kindness towards her. Nothing warms a mother's heart more than seeing her husband interacting with the children in positive ways.

Ironically, it is often the smaller acts of kindness that mean the most. We sometimes fall into the trap of believing that, because we work hard every day to provide for the family, we are exempt from showing common courtesies and simple kindnesses.

That isn't true.

Providing for your children's physical needs is only part of the picture. Sure, they need food on the table and a roof over their head, but they also need your patience and prayers and protection. They long for you to be involved and invested in their lives—taking pride in their accomplishments, praising each step of progress, offering pointers for improvement, and being present, interested, and available whenever they need you.

Your kids want to please you. Be sure to let them know when they do!

"I cannot think of any need in childhood as strong as the need for a father's protection."

- Sigmund Freud

Although it is important that we deal swiftly and consistently with our children's wrongful behavior, it's equally important to acknowledge and encourage their good behavior with sincere and appropriate praise.

Doing so takes a lot of patience.

We discussed showing patience toward your wife at length in the last chapter, but your children need that tender resolution and understanding just as much as your spouse does.

Patience toward them comes in two varieties: The first is in dealing with the day-to-day stuff that can really get on your nerves. The second really is more in the category of perseverance and involves hanging in there for years at a time while your child slowly finds their place in the world. When you do this, when you consciously and consistently invest time and energy in your offspring, you are investing in your wife as well.

Children spell quality time: Q-U-A-N-T-I-T-Y. Be intentional about establishing everyday routines with your kids, as well as creating special memories with them. When we tend to the hours and the days, the years take care of themselves. Thus, we should pray with the Psalmist,

> *"Teach us to number our days, that we may present to You a heart of wisdom."*
>
> (Psalm 90:12, NASB)

That old adage you see on bumper stickers and greeting cards may be corny, but it's true: Any man can be a father, but it takes someone special to be a dad. Devote yourself to being the best dad you can be. The more love you lavish on your children, the more will spill over on your wife.

Put It into Practice:

✍ Play games with your children. Take delight in their company. This can take the form of board games like checkers, chess, or Chutes & Ladders, or it can mean a rousing game of hide & seek, tag, or tickle chase (cue the childish laughter, because there's sure to be a lot of it).

✍ Teach your children sports basics: show them how to toss a Frisbee, kick a soccer ball, shoot hoops, and pitch a softball.

✍ If you are handy in the kitchen, teach your kids how to make pancakes, cook dinner, or prepare hot tea. Bring a cup to Mama, so she can rave over the results, as well.

✍ Are you mechanically inclined? Show your children how to replace a bike tire, tune up the lawn mower, change the oil, plunge a toilet, and do simple home repairs. These are great life skills for anybody to have, so be sure you teach your daughters as well as your sons.

✍ If you are artistic, pass that knowledge along to your children, as well. Let them try their hand at painting or sculpting or sketching or woodwork. Sing and make music together at every opportunity.

✍ When you've errands to run, bring a child along for the ride. You'll be amazed at what you can learn by chatting in the car on the way to the cleaners.

Choose Her
over Hobbies
or Buddies

Chapter 19

Invariably there will come times in your relationship when you will be forced to choose between your wife and something else that you enjoy.

Always choose her.

Yes, I understand that friends and hobbies are important. I'm NOT saying you must eliminate them. It is possible to enjoy hobbies (in moderation) or to spend time with buddies (occasionally) and *still* remain happily married.

What I AM saying is this: Whenever you find yourself facing an either/or decision—a decision where you must decide between your wife and some other temporal pleasure—go with your wife.

Let me give an example. You've made it five years, and your anniversary falls on a Wednesday. Unbeknownst to you, your wife has arranged a surprise romantic dinner at her favorite restaurant and is hoping to discuss the possibility of starting a family in the near future.

Unfortunately, Wednesday is also the night of the fantasy football league draft in the man-cave at your best friend's house. Guy thinking says to push the anniversary celebration to Friday and enjoy the best of both worlds. *Win-win.*

> "The relationship between husband and wife should be one of closest friends."
>
> - B.R. Ambedkar

I'm saying, *don't do it.* Don't even let on that you are conflicted about it! Give your draft picks to your buddy, hope for the best, and celebrate your anniversary. Then, for bonus points, have your friend leave a message on your answering machine saying he'll miss you at the draft, but respects the fact that your wife is way more important to you than football.

Which, hopefully, is true!

Prioritizing time with your wife over time spent on hobbies and buddies is a great way to communicate how important she is to you.

- If your goal is to show your wife that you love her, you should "always" choose her.
- If your goal is to aggravate her, then you should "always" choose the something else.

- If your goal is to keep her guessing about your loyalty, then you should mix it up a little: Your BFF takes precedence over her, but so-so friends don't.

Of course, there will sometimes be emergencies or other extenuating circumstances that force you to put time with your wife on the back burner—but that kind of thing should be a rarity.

Also, the amount of free time available to divvy up will undoubtedly affect how you spend it, as well.

When I was in my residency training, it was not unusual for me to be kept at the hospital 120 hours a week, leaving only a few wakeful hours for me to spend with my family. If I'd chosen to spend what little free time I had shooting hoops with my buddies instead of investing in the lives of my wife and children, it would have sent a clear message to my family that they were about as low on my list of priorities as they could be.

> "Good things happen when you get your priorities straight."
>
> - Scott Caan

Now that I'm in practice and have more control over the hours I work, I can squeeze in a little three-on-three after dinner and story time without alienating my wife or neglecting my children whatsoever (in fact, my older sons are often on the court— or at the Ping-Pong tables or on the Frisbee field—with me).

But had my wife made secret, special plans that conflicted with our father/son sports, I'd choose her.

Put It into Practice:

✍ Which of your hobbies are most likely to encroach upon time with your wife? Is there a way you can involve her in the hobby and work together? Doing so can turn either/or propositions into both/and opportunities.

✍ Friends are important, but if you are constantly forgoing couple time to hang out with your buddies while she spends time with her girlfriends, then you are probably pouring too much time and energy into secondary relationships and not enough into your marriage. Scale back on extracurricular activities that separate you in favor of spending more time as a couple. Develop friendships with other married couples who share your values and vision, so that you can all challenge and support one another.

✍ Ask your wife whether she resents any of the activities to which you devote your free time. Many a wife has felt like a widow during hunting or football season, or when her husband becomes over-involved in (read: addicted to) video games. If she thinks the amount of time you spend on a given hobby is a problem, then it's a problem. Listen to her and make any necessary adjustments.

Provide for
Her Needs

Chapter 20

"But if anyone does not provide for his own, and especially for those of his house, he has denied the faith and is worse than an unbeliever." (1 Timothy 5:8, NASB)

Paul certainly takes a hard line on the subject of provision for one's family. "Worse than an unbeliever" is probably the most severe insult possible from Paul's perspective, but he doesn't pull any punches.

I guess it just shows that "dead-beat dads" have been around for thousands of years. In the last few generations, however, this type of behavior seems to have escalated.

Historically, a man only took a wife when he was ready to support and provide for her, as well as any children who might come along.

In today's age of dual-income families, the notion of the husband as breadwinner will strike many as dated and quaint. Yet, even though a wife's work (whether in or out of the home, financially compensated or not) contributes significantly to a household's bottom line, it is squarely upon the man's shoulders that Scripture places the responsibility of making certain his family is well provisioned. That is the Biblical ideal, and should be our goal, as well.

Before I go into detail about what it means to provide, I want to address the issue of disability.

As a physician who has served in the military myself and has been called upon to conduct disability evaluations for a number of public and private institutions, I am well acquainted with this subject.

> "Everyone needs a house to live in, but a supportive family is what builds a home."
>
> - Anthony Liccione

"Disability" is a very broad term. One size does not fit all. I've known soldiers in a rush to get their prosthetic limbs properly fitted so that they could hurry and get back to work. As I write, the governor of Texas serves our great state from a wheelchair. FDR governed the nation in similar fashion.

Unfortunately, I have also seen a wide variety of attempts to "game the system" by physically healthy people trying to get something for nothing.

Chapter 20 – Provide for Her Needs

If you are truly disabled, please utilize all the resources, public and private, available to you. The safety nets that society has put in place are there for you. Use them. There is no shame in using them. They are a legitimate way to provide for both yourself and your dependents.

If you happen to be a soldier, police officer, fireman, or other public servant who was injured in the line of duty, thank you for your service and your sacrifice. We should honor you more than we do.

If, on the other hand, you are healthy and are taking advantage of either your employer or the government illegitimately, you are stealing from those truly in need.

I doubt you would dump a crippled person out of their wheelchair onto the floor so that you could use it to go joyriding down the hallway while the rightful owner lay crumpled in a heap. Yet, in effect, that is what you are doing if you accept disability assistance when you don't have a legitimate need for it. You should be ashamed, and you shouldn't rest until you've made the situation right.

"Don't let what you can't do define you; rather, let it refine you, molding you into a better provider in other ways."

- Doug Flanders

The good news is that regardless of your health status or your ability to provide financially, finances are only one aspect of provision. Sometimes when we are lacking in one arena, we can find ways to compensate in another. Don't let what you can't do define you; rather, let it refine you, molding you into a better provider in other ways.

Your wife has spiritual, intellectual, emotional, familial, social, and physical needs. I will address each of these in turn and then discuss finances in greater detail. In particular, I would like to look at the question, "How much is enough?"

Let's start at the top with spiritual provision.

Spiritual Provision

Typically women are more spiritually sensitive than men, yet husbands are the ones to whom God gives the responsibility of leading in this area. I have already discussed the importance of prayer in marriage, but what about studying the Bible with your family?

> "Great leaders don't make excuses. They make things better. They are not unrealistic or blind to the difficulties they face. They simply are not discouraged by them."
>
> - Henry Blackaby

I set aside a few minutes each evening to read aloud from a children's Bible and discuss the stories with our kids. It isn't much, but a little done consistently is better than a lot done sporadically: In this way, we are teaching them *"precept upon precept, precept upon precept, line upon line, line upon line, here a little, there a little."* (Isaiah 28:10, ESV) Then the bigger activities and the longer studies simply become bonuses!

How about church attendance? Do you send your wife and children to attend without you? Why not join them and worship as a family? What about service projects and missions trips? They can be great bonding experiences, as well a good opportunity to serve others in need.

There are lots of ways to provide spiritually. Ask God to open your eyes to them and give you the will to follow through.

Intellectual Provision

Intellectual provision can mean a variety of things. It may simply be providing your wife with adult conversation after she's spent a long day chasing little ones around the house. It might also mean helping your wife finish her college degree.

No one wants to stagnate mentally. We are all driven to grow and learn. Do what you can to help your wife expand her horizons and fulfill this God-given aspect of her humanity.

I have one friend who got married straight out of high school with the intention of being a stay at home mom. Now she is a physician who specializes in robotic surgery! I also know teachers, nurses, lawyers, and a variety of other

> "Try to learn something about everything and everything about something."
>
> - Thomas Huxley

professionals, who got their degrees "once the kids were grown."

Your wife is unique. What intellectual challenge or fulfillment looks like for her will be different from anyone else. It's your job to be sensitive to that and to help her when it is at all possible to do so.

Emotional Provision

Emotional provision is a difficult one. Some wives are very needy in this area. Some are not. However, even the most stoic of wives longs to be loved and appreciated.

A calm demeanor doesn't indicate a lack of need, just a better set of coping skills. In either case, love your wife, and then reassure her of your love in both word and deed as often as you can and in every way you can.

Familial Provision

Familial provision acknowledges the fact that your wife may also be a mother, a sister, a daughter, a granddaughter, a cousin, or you name it.

> "To us, family means putting our arms around each other and being there."
>
> - Barbara Bush

Those titles come with some responsibilities, and it is your duty to help her fulfill them. You didn't just marry her; you married her family. In some families this is an easy and pleasant task, in others, it is not.

Do your best. If it is hard on you, it is even harder

on her, because she is the one with the relationships to maintain. As with her children, kindness to her extended family translates into kindness to her.

Social Provision

Social provision means your wife has friends. You may not like some of those friends. She may not like your friends, either.

Do what you can to be a peacemaker.

Some friendships may need to be sacrificed for the good of the marriage, but this should be the exception, not the rule. Allow her to spend time with her friends, online, on the phone, or in person. You may need to agree on some boundaries, but avoid ultimatums.

Financial Provision

So now we are back to finances. That subject could fill not only a whole book, but also a whole section of a bookstore. I won't try to reproduce all that wisdom here, but I will point out a few rules of thumb that may help keep you out of trouble.

Of course, we must first recognize the fact that it is God who ultimately provides for all of us:

- *"As for the rich in this present age, charge them not to be haughty, nor to set their hopes on the uncertainty of riches, but on God, who richly provides us with everything to enjoy."* (1 Timothy 6:17, NIV)
- *"I was young and now I am old, yet I have never seen the righteous forsaken or their children begging bread."* (Psalm 37:25, NIV)

121

- *"And my God will supply all your needs according to His riches in glory in Christ Jesus."* (Philippians 4:19, NASB)
- *"The eyes of all look to You, and You give them their food in due time. You open Your hand and satisfy the desire of every living thing."* (Psalm 145:15-16, NASB)
- *"And God will generously provide all you need. Then you will always have everything you need and plenty left over to share with others."* (2 Corinthians 9:8, NLT)

Ultimately, God provides, but He normally uses human agency to do it. "God helps those who help themselves," while technically not a Bible verse, is an accurate observation nonetheless.

Working hard is always a win.

If you are watching a baseball game and the outfielder dives for the ball, then at least you know he is trying, even if he misses the catch. If he just stands there whistling while the ball whizzes past, you will be furious, even though the result is the same.

> "Perseverance is the hard work you do after you get tired of doing the hard work you already did."
>
> - Newt Gingrich

Effort is every bit as important, if not more so, than outcome.

Everyone respects a diligent worker, including your wife. She will be willing to live with less, as long as she knows you are trying.

Chapter 20 – Provide for Her Needs

If you are already working as hard as you can and barely making ends meet, then you may need to learn to work smarter. Get some education. This doesn't have to be formal education, but very likely it will be.

There are some two-year associate degrees that will leapfrog your income over that of many people with Master's degrees and even doctorates. Furthermore, some technical certifications are every bit as valuable as a college degree. Get some guidance, then get after it.

Then you and your family can stop living with less, and just start living.

Consider taking one of Dave Ramsey's money management courses. He summarizes all the basic stuff you need to know in a nice, concise, and easy to understand way. I will leave it to him to tell you not to buy stuff you don't need or get too deeply in debt and that sort of thing.

> "An investment in knowledge pays the best interest."
>
> - Benjamin Franklin

If you are working hard and working smart, then managing that income wisely is the next logical step. If you do that, then you are providing for the future and for all the "what if's" life can throw at you. Money management is as important a facet of financial provision as making the money in the first place.

Finally, you must also learn to manage your life well. Money really isn't everything. The trick is to know, "How much is enough?"

Studies have shown that, in America, average happiness increases with rising income up until about seventy thousand dollars of income per household per year, then after that, happiness levels begin to decline.[1]

Beyond a certain level, the act of earning more actually erodes the benefits of having more. Where that break point is for your family is something you will have to discover for yourself—hopefully not the hard way.

Sometimes, less really is more.

As we've seen, "providing for her needs" means much more than just putting food on the table. It is all encompassing. On the one hand, basic human needs remain the same from person to person and culture to culture: We all need to eat, to sleep, to have friendships and a sense of purpose, to give and receive love. But on the other hand, We are each unique individuals with variability in what foods taste good to us, what things we perceive as beautiful, what we think is important, or even what we think is fun.

> "A little thought and a little kindness are often worth more than a great deal of money."
>
> - John Ruskin

Part of the enjoyment of marriage is discovering those unique needs in our spouse and meeting them in unique ways. Sometimes—by God's grace—our abilities match the challenge, but sometimes our abilities need to be built up or bolstered, which has the advantage of growing us in the process.

Your family is counting on you. Whether you're addressing physical needs, social needs, emotional needs, spiritual needs, familial needs or any other kind of need—do your best to provide, trusting God to bless your efforts.

124

Put It into Practice:

✍ What are some ways you can increase your earning potential? Is it time to sign up for an online class? Or go through that certification course at work? Maybe even go back and get that MBA you've been thinking about?

✍ A penny saved is actually closer to *two* pennies earned, in that you won't be required to pay taxes on it. Spending less means you need to earn less. Brainstorm with your wife about creative ways to cut expenses.

✍ What about the other side of the coin? Are you a workaholic? Perhaps you would be better served in your marriage by earning a little less and focusing on other ways to provide for your wife's needs.

✍ What is your wife's greatest need? It may not be what you think. Perhaps a frank discussion with her would be a good starting point.

Dial Down
the Anger

Chapter 21

Your caveman instincts may be handy on the battlefield, but they're horrible for a happy home life. Every outburst or flare-up is a relationship setback.

Just because your wife puts up with it and your co-workers tolerate it, does not make your short fuse an asset. You must do whatever it takes to gain victory in this all-important struggle that has haunted man since Cain slew Abel.

The first step in moving forward is to stop going backwards. You must learn to control your temper or it will control you, your marriage, and every other aspect of your life.

The Bible has a lot to say about anger, much of it warning us of the destruction that awaits the person who allows himself to be ruled by a fiery temper:

- *"A fool gives full vent to his anger, but a wise man keeps himself under control."* (Proverbs 29:11, NIV)
- *"He who is slow to anger has great understanding, But he who is quick-tempered exalts folly."* (Proverbs 14:29, NASB)
- *"Put them all aside: anger, wrath, malice, slander, and abusive speech from your mouth."* (Colossians 3:8, NASB)
- *"A hot-tempered person stirs up conflict, but the one who is patient calms a quarrel."* (Proverbs 15:18, NIV)
- *"But everyone must be quick to hear, slow to speak and slow to anger; for the anger of man does not achieve the righteousness of God."* (James 1:19-20, NASB)

I once overheard some coworkers discussing a friend of mine. Although they weren't talking about me, they easily could have been. What they had to say was this: "He's the nicest guy you'd ever want to meet—right up until he isn't."

> **"Whatever is begun in anger ends in shame."**
>
> - Benjamin Franklin

Their assessment was spot on. Not just of my friend, but of many people, including myself.

My wife describes it as living on an island with an active volcano.

Chapter 21 – Dial Down the Anger

You've seen the pictures: Lush, vibrant, and beautiful, it's a tropical paradise in all directions. Yet there, at the top of the rise, you spot the glowing mouth of a volcano, ready and waiting to spew forth its molten lava at any moment, unbidden and unexpected.

Sometimes there are little tremors that let those who live nearby know it's coming, but it's usually at its worst when it blows without warning.

When my wife and I first married, unbeknownst to either of us, I was harboring an anger problem. A ferocious, fiery temper that had lain dormant for

> "Anger dwells only in the bosom of fools."
>
> - Albert Einstein

years was now erupting suddenly, violently, and with alarming regularity any time the pressures below the surface exceeded the limits of containment.

Although I never laid a hand on my wife during those fits of rage, our china dishes didn't fare so well. It began with a broken saucer here or there and culminated with a full plate of spaghetti thrown against the dining room wall. However, it wasn't until I punched a hole in our bedroom wall—an ill-advised act that left small but permanent scars on my right hand—that I was finally able to see just how serious my problem had become.

I had to change.

That much was obvious. My marriage would never be the happy union I desired, nor would my children grow up to be the kind of people I'd want them to be, unless I could be the kind of person I ought to be.

But how?

Like so many addicts of other types, I was forced to admit I had a problem and was powerless to fix it on my own. My anger would require divine intervention.

So I prayed.

In abject humility and desperation, I begged God to change my heart—if not for my sake, at least for the sake of my wife and children.

> "When anger rises, think of the consequences."
>
> - Confucius

And answer my prayer, He did.

Most people who know me today find this tale almost implausible. They have a hard time imagining me ever hurling plates or putting my fist through a wall.

Although I can still get a little testy from time to time, my temper is nothing like it was—or might still be, apart from God's transformative help.

But a few flare-ups and knuckle scars aren't my only reminders. My sweet, insightful wife saved all the tiny pieces of those broken china dishes and used them to create a mosaic mirror frame to hang in our home. Whenever I look at that mirror, I am able to reflect on where I've been and see clearly where I'm hoping to go.

The mirror is deeply symbolic.

My wife's taking what I had ruined and making something pretty from it serves as an analogy for what God does on a much grander scale. He delights in taking the shattered, broken pieces of our lives and fashioning something breathtakingly beautiful from them. He has done that for me, and He will do it for you, provided you are willing to entrust all the fragments and splintered shards to His care.

If you struggle with anger (or with any other problem), don't try to hide it or justify it or marginalize the damage that it's doing to your life and loved ones. Face up to the problem and seek help from the only One who can change hearts.

Stop Making Excuses

The biggest mistake people make is trying to explain away their anger. In intellectual circles, this takes the form of the "survival advantage" of anger. Norwegians in particular, of whom I am descended, were known for their fearsome Vikings, including a special breed known as "Berserkers."

Unlike warriors who wanted to fight all the time or pacifists who couldn't defend themselves, berserkers kept the crazy in balance (most of the time). They could hold down a normal job, interact with polite society, and carry on like normal people until faced with some looming threat that flipped the switch.

Once triggered, berserkers would become bloodthirsty killing machines that were nearly invincible in battle. The problem was that they were sometimes triggered when there was no battle to be had. They were great during war. Not so great the rest of the time.

Yet scientists would have us believe the raging temper of a berserker was a

> "Anger is a wind which blows out the lamp of the mind."
>
> - Robert Green Ingersoll

positive trait that helped him survive in a hostile environment.

In Christian circles, the justification follows a different vein. Unsurprising, it is a more spiritual one. When some men are confronted about their anger issues, they try to explain it away by claiming theirs is a "righteous anger." They are quick to recount the story of Jesus driving the moneychangers from the temple and argue unconvincingly that the spilled milkshake or the stalled car or the spouse's simple statement is a comparable situation in their case.

Few people are willing to call anger what it is, which is sin. The scientifically minded want to deny sin exists *at all*; the spiritually minded refuse to admit sin exists *in them*. But spiritualizing anger or explaining it away are not the only ways we attempt to justify losing our tempers. The most common response is to blame someone else.

> "Anger is never without a reason, but seldom with a good one."
>
> - Benjamin Franklin

When I was a young doctor in training, I once worked with a surgeon who was struggling to carry out a particular procedure. As the case went on, he became more and more agitated and began unleashing his vehemence on various staff members in the operating room. Realizing he had more frustration than helpers, he then began calling additional people into the room so that he could give them a piece of his mind, as well.

When he finally ran out of people to harangue, he turned his gaze upon me.

"Dr. Flanders," he began solemnly.

Chapter 21 – Dial Down the Anger

"Yes," I answered, a smile forming under my mask as I wondered what pretense he might use to yell at me.

"I want you to know—it's *not me*," he explained a little sheepishly. "It's *everyone else!*"

"Okay," I answered, the hidden grin spreading across my face. Perhaps he sensed my mirth, or simply realized the absurdity of his statement, but the room was quiet for the rest of the case.

I've seen similar scenarios played out in the past twenty-some-odd years. Although no surgeon since has had the audacity to say it, their message is still loud and clear: *"It's not me—it's everyone else!"*

The sad truth is, anger is rarely about everybody else. Life is full of frustration. You can bank on it. The question is not whether we'll ever face troubles, but how we'll respond to those troubles when they come.

This concept is every bit as true in marriage as it is in the operating room. I can't tell you how many men would rather talk about their wife's issues than address this one, even when it is staring them right in the face.

> **"Speak when you are angry— and you'll make the best speech you'll ever regret."**
>
> - Laurence Peter

When a fellow I knew to be hot-tempered asked me once for some generic marriage advice, I casually mentioned what a glaring problem anger is for many husbands. In response, he became quite red in the face and emphatically insisted, "*She's* the one with an anger problem, not *me!*"

He then provided several examples that painted him to be a saint and his wife to be fatally flawed.

"Then it sounds like she's the one who needs marriage advice," I told him dryly, "since you're obviously doing so well."

Missing any hint of sarcasm, he heartedly agreed with this assessment, and our conversation ended.

This pattern seems to be the rule rather than the exception. We are quick to point out our spouse's shortcomings, but slow to claim our own. Granted, there are faults to be found on both sides of the fence, but yours are the only ones over which you have any measure of control.

> "There was never an angry man that thought his anger unjust."
>
> - Saint Francis de Sales

It's time to exercise that control. Leave God to deal with your wife's anger issues. By His enabling grace, you must focus on addressing your own.

Stop blaming your foul temper on the fact that you are tired or stressed or hungry or irritated by noisy kids or a messy house. There is no good excuse, no rational justification for sin.

None of those things absolve you of the responsibility of bridling your tongue and keeping your temper in check.

Put It into Practice:

✍ In what circumstances are you most prone to become angry or lose your temper? Think through your reactions beforehand. What would be a better response? Rehearse that response in your mind and pray that God will help you resist falling back into your old sin patterns next time you find yourself in a similar predicament.

✍ When you do trip up, be the first to apologize. (But if your wife, bless her heart, beats you to it and apologizes first, don't take that as your cue to launch into the second half of your tirade.)

✍ James 3:18 tells us, "The seed whose fruit is righteousness is sown in peace by those who make peace." What steps can you take to be more of a peacemaker in your home?

✍ Don't underestimate the power of prayer to change engrained habits. God can make something beautiful out of even the most (seemingly) hopeless situations. What is keeping you from turning the broken fragments of your life over to Him?

Cut Out
the
Condescension

Chapter 22

If you have been blessed with a quick wit, you can either be the life of the party or a pain in the neck, depending on the circumstances.

Condescension is anger's younger brother. It isn't as loud or as dramatic, but it can be equally hurtful, and all the more so for its subtlety. Whether you realize it or not, condescension springs from pride and communicates contempt—two attitudes that have dealt the death blow to many a marriage.

So lay off the snide remarks, the sarcasm, and the belittling. Speak to your wife the way you would a respected colleague. She is, after all, your partner in the most valuable investment of your life—your family.

When it comes to disdainful speech, Scripture sets a zero-tolerance policy:

> *"Do not let **any** unwholesome talk come out of your mouths, but **only** what is helpful for building others up according to their needs, that it may benefit those who listen."*
>
> (Ephesians 4:29, NIV—emphasis added)

The reason "Cut out the Condescension" even appears on this 25-ways list? Because this is something I often struggle with myself.

Sometimes I can be a real jerk.

And once I climb up on my high horse, I have a hard time getting down.

In the early days of my marriage, I camped out up there a good deal of the time. My wife would say or do something that set me off, and I would launch into an hour-long diatribe and wouldn't stop until I had painstakingly dissected, then laid out in order, every minute detail of whatever mistake she'd made—real or imagined, past, present, or future.

> "When it comes to disdainful speech, Scripture sets a zero-tolerance policy."
>
> - Doug Flanders

It's a wonder she stuck with me through all the nonsense I dished out as a new husband.

During the decades that followed, I calmed down considerably. My belabored lectures are much more of a rarity these days—she gets one or two a year now instead of one or two a day—and they are not nearly as caustic as they once were, thanks to the abundant grace of God (and my wife's thoughtful avoidance of well-documented triggers).

Still, the damage done during those occasional slips by my words and tone and attitudes can have lingering ill effects. Condescension crushes fellowship. It erodes trust and creates unnecessary obstacles that must later be hurdled if unity is to be restored.

When it's directed at our wives, it also compromises our testimony, insofar as it fails to reflect the pure, self-sacrificing love Christ has for the church—the love God calls husbands to model.

As with any bad habit, the first step in conquering and cutting out condescension is to admit there's a problem. We must call it what it is: *sin*. There's no other word for it.

When we allow our tongue or our tone to tear others down instead of building them up, we are doing wrong. The Bible is clear on that fact:

> "Condescension crushes fellowship, erodes trust, and creates unnecessary obstacles that must later be hurdled if unity is to be restored."
>
> - Doug Flanders

- *"When there are many words, transgression is unavoidable, but he who restrains his lips is wise."* (Proverbs 10:19, NASB)

- *"It's not what goes into your mouth that defiles you; you are defiled by the words that come out of your mouth."* (Matthew 15:11, NLT)
- *"Those who guard their lips preserve their lives, but those who speak rashly will come to ruin."* (Proverbs 13:3, NIV)
- *"Those who consider themselves religious and yet do not keep a tight rein on their tongues deceive themselves, and their religion is worthless."* (James 1:26, NIV)
- *"If you want to enjoy life and see many happy days, keep your tongue from speaking evil and your lips from telling lies."* (1 Peter 3:10, NLT)
- *"The good man brings out of his good treasure what is good; and the evil man brings out of his evil treasure what is evil. But I tell you that every careless word that people speak, they shall give an accounting for it in the day of judgment. For by your words you will be justified, and by your words you will be condemned."* (Matthew 12:35-37, NASB)
- *"So also the tongue is a small part of the body, and yet it boasts of great things. See how great a forest is set aflame by such a small fire! And the tongue is a fire, the very world of iniquity; the tongue is set among our members as that which defiles the entire body, and sets on fire the course of our life, and is set on fire by hell."* (James 3:5-6, NASB)

Again, it may not be the content of what you are saying that is the problem. It may be the attitude with which you say it.

Chapter 22 – Cut Out the Condensation

A condescending tone will make it virtually impossible for your wife to appreciate the wisdom of your words. Like a ring of gold in a pig's snout, the truth will be muddied, if not completely obscured, by your offensive attitude and repulsive manner.

If your wife has been blessed with an extra measure of self-confidence, she may be able to weather your verbal or insinuated attack on her self-worth and intelligence, although such a climate certainly won't help her flourish.

If, on the other hand, your beloved struggles with self-doubt or with other insecurities already, your condescension can destroy her. Certainly, it can destroy your marriage.

> "What are others worth, that they have the nerve to sneer at any human being?"
>
> - Graham Greene

Don't let it.

It is time that we cut out condescension with the same comprehensive thoroughness that a cancer surgeon uses to excise a malignant tumor. For a malignancy it is, and one we can't afford to ignore any longer.

Put It into Practice:

✍ Do your words and tone make your wife feel cherished and respected? Scripture urges us to *"outdo one another in showing honor."* (Romans 12:10, ESV) You want your wife to speak respectfully to you. Why not lead by example?

✍ Next time you catch yourself edging toward condescension in a conversation, *STOP*. Go to God in prayer. Confess your pride. Ask for grace. Hold your tongue until you can say what needs to be said with a respectful tone, always and only *"speaking the truth in love."* (Ephesians 4:15, NASB)

✍ It may be that your wife and children have sensed condescension where none was intended. Ask them to point out to you tones, phrases, and attitudes that make them feel demeaned, then resolve, by God's grace, to stop using such methods of communication in future conversations.

Actively Seek
Your Wife's
Insights

Chapter 23

The one measureable variable that correlates most strongly between married couples is IQ.[1] We tend to be attracted to people to whom we can relate, so statistically speaking, there's a high probability that your wife is just as smart as you are.

Value her input and give it a preferential place in your decision making process. Women are masters of communication and of multi-tasking, and therefore bring a unique feminine perspective to every challenge.

The Bible teaches that, where there is a multitude of counselors, plans succeed and wisdom prevails:

- *"Plans fail for lack of counsel, but with many advisers they succeed."* (Proverbs 15:22, NIV)

- *"Prepare plans by consultation, and make war by wise guidance."*(Proverbs 20:18, NASB)
- *"The way of fools seem right to them, but the wise listen to advice."* (Proverbs 12:15, NIV)
- *"Where no counsel is, the people fall: but in the multitude of counselors there is safety."* (Proverbs 11:14, KJV)

Granted, two is not a multitude, but it's a start.

Historically, it's been very common for married scientists to collaborate. Think Pierre and Marie Curie. Irene and Frederic Joliot-Curie. Carl and Gerty Cori. All three of these couples were awarded Nobel prizes for their collaborative contributions to science.[2] Each of these men placed a high value on his wife's insights and observations, with life-changing and world-enriching results.

> "Two are better than one, because they have a good return for their labor."
>
> - Ecclesiastes 4:9, NIV

Likewise, writers almost universally use their spouses as first-line editors. This is certainly true in my case, but is also characteristic of far more famous and successful writers, including Dostoevsky, Stephen King, and Paul Krugman (another Nobel prize winner). Tolstoy's wife Sofya famously copied his 560,000-word *War and Peace* by hand eight times (and still found time to bear him 13 children).[3]

Beyond the practical side of things, there remains the fact that your spouse will be heavily influenced and affected by the decisions you make—good or bad—and deserves the right to have input accordingly. When you marry, you give up a certain amount of autonomy. Like every trade-off, it has pros and cons, but it is the reality, nonetheless.

Perhaps this is what Peter had in mind when he advised husbands to "live with [their] wives in an understanding way." (1 Peter 3:7, ESV)

When you do ask for your wife's insight or opinion, try not to immediately shoot down her ideas. Don't become overly critical or defensive. Just *listen.*

Give thoughtful consideration to her words. Examine and evaluate every point she makes. Pray about the matter. And incorporate her ideas whenever you can and wherever it makes sense to do so.

If you are negligent in this area—if you refuse to consult your wife before making major decisions or to carefully consider her unique perspective—then you are effectively wasting a resource God fully intended for you to utilize. He has designed husband and wife to complement one another, not only physically, but emotionally and intellectually, as well.

> "The single biggest problem in communication is the illusion that it has taken place."
>
> - George Bernard Shaw

Put It into Practice:

✍ Wondering where to start on seeking input from your wife? How about asking her how she thinks you're doing in your role as a husband and father? Tell her you want her to be completely honest with you. Ask her to identify the areas that need the most attention, and see if she has suggestions as to how you might improve.

✍ Ask your wife to pray for you as you work to make the aforementioned improvements, then revisit the topic later so she can evaluate your progress.

✍ I'm a little bit of an impulsive shopper. I frequently purchase things that find their way to Goodwill within a few short weeks of my bringing them home, once I realize I don't need/like/use something as much as I thought I would when I bought it. Since my wife can usually and accurately predict which things I'll hold onto and which I'll likely toss, we stay dollars ahead when I consult her before buying. Are there any areas like this in your life? Sometimes our wives know us better than we know ourselves. How can you make best use of that knowledge?

Learn to Forgive

Chapter 24

Jesus tells the story of a slave who was forgiven a great debt by his master. The slave went out and almost immediately began beating a fellow slave in an attempt to extract a much smaller debt. Needless to say the master was not pleased to discover the first slave's merciless behavior.

Yet, how often do we act just like that ungrateful slave when it comes to sin?

Invariably, we want mercy for ourselves, but justice for everyone else. The things that ensnare us always seem *so minor* compared to the heinous crimes committed by our fellow man.

Jesus's message was clear: Stop beating the other slaves! Learn to forgive, just as you have been forgiven.

Forgiveness is at the heart of the gospel and the heart of every healthy relationship. This is especially true of the marriage relationship. The sheer volume of time a husband and wife spend together, day after day, year after year, translates into ample opportunity both to offend and to take offense.

> "Don't brood. Get on with living and loving. You don't have forever."
>
> - Leo Buscaglia

Your marriage will never thrive—and it may not even survive—unless you can learn how to forgive. A successful marriage, Ruth Bell Graham reminds us, "is the union of two good forgivers."

I believe that's true.

What follows are six principles that have been helpful to me in seeking and extending forgiveness to both my wife and others:

1. **When requesting forgiveness of anybody, we should always begin with God.**

   Ultimately, all sin is an affront to Him. We must go to Him first. The price has already been paid through Christ's blood. We must repent of our sin and ask Him to help as we seek forgiveness from others. (Psalm 51:1-4; 1 John 1:9)

2. When seeking forgiveness from others, we must be prepared to make restitution.

Sometimes seeking forgiveness requires more than just saying I'm sorry. We should convey sincere remorse for the wrongs we have done, certainly, but we must also seek to make amends to the best of our abilities and to the degree that restitution is possible. (Numbers 5:7)

3. When extending forgiveness to others, we should work towards restoration.

Ideally, forgiveness is just the first step in restoring a broken relationship. When grudges are held, the relationship suffers or is non-existent. Forgiveness allows healing to begin. It is like draining an emotional abscess. The only true way to conquer an enemy is to make him a friend. (Luke 17:3-4; Galatians 6:1)

4. When restoration is impossible, forgiveness is still important.

Even if the person we need to forgive is dead or in jail, forgiveness still has its place. Learning to forgive others is as much for our own benefit as it is for theirs. Maybe even more. (Mark 11:25; Ephesians 4:31-32)

"When you forgive, you in no way change the past— but you sure do change the future."

- Bernard Meltzer

5. When walking in God's forgiveness, we need to also forgive ourselves.

Sometimes this is the hardest thing to do. We may have asked God's forgiveness and even made restitution, but we just can't let it go. We must stop beating ourselves up! Self-flagellation is not only unhealthy on multiple levels, but it implies that Christ's sacrifice on the cross was insufficient. (Romans 8:1; Psalm 103:12)

6. To live a life of forgiveness, we must learn to forgive God.

This may seem like a strange concept, but look around. The world is full of people who are angry with God. Perhaps they are angry about the way He made them: Too short or too tall, too skinny or too fat, ears too big or feet too small, no good at math or music or sports.

> "To forgive
> is to set
> a prisoner free
> and discover
> that the prisoner
> was you."
>
> - Lewis B. Smedes

Perhaps they're angry about their life circumstances (often understandably so!): Why did I get laid off from that job I loved? Why did my spouse leave me after twenty years? Why did my sister die so young?

They reason that if God is ultimately in control, then He is ultimately to blame. We may never have intellectually framed it in those terms, but emotionally we all need to forgive God for something.

Such forgiveness can only spring from the knowledge that God has a purpose and plan for our life and the confidence that He will work even bad things together for our good and His glory. If we are harboring bitterness and resentment against God for perceived wrongdoings of any kind, the real problem lies not in His actions toward us, but in our attitude toward Him. (Romans 9:20; Jeremiah 29:11; Romans 8:28)

And thus we have come full circle. The list begins with God and ends with God, just as all things do. (Revelation 1:8)

The good news is that once we've learned to "forgive" God, we actually begin to trust Him.

As our trust in Him grows, we one day find that we are learning to love Him just as He loves us. It is a love rooted in forgiveness, and that love and forgiveness can then spill over onto our fellow man, so that these principles really start to become second nature. (2 Corinthians 5:17)

> "There is no love without forgiveness, and there is no forgiveness without love."
>
> - Bryant H. McGill

151

Put It into Practice:

✍ Imagine that your wife has apologized for something she said or did that upset you. You said you forgave her, but every time you think about the incident, you begin to get angry or irritated all over again—even weeks (or months or years) later. Has that ever happened to you? If so, you can be pretty certain you never completely forgave her in the first place. "Forgiveness is not an occasional act," observed Martin Luther King, "it is a constant attitude." Use your angry irritation as a signal to lay the matter back at the foot of the Cross and to ask for God's help in leaving it there.

✍ If you realize that you have offended your wife by some thoughtless word or deed, do not waste time trying to justify or defend or excuse your actions. Instead, apologize sincerely and immediately, and purpose to avoid such behavior in the future.

✍ Memorize Colossians 3:13: *"Make allowance for each other's faults, and forgive anyone who offends you. Remember, the Lord forgave you, so you must forgive others."* Do your best to daily live this verse out in your home.

✍ Look up other Bible verses referenced in this chapter and spend some time meditating on them. Commit a few to memory and endeavor to follow the principles taught in your daily walk.

Verbally
Express
Your Love

Chapter 25

When my wife and I first published our *25 Ways* posts shortly after our 25th wedding anniversary, I drew criticism for making love the focus of my list, rather than respect. This offended some of my readers, who (rightly) felt that women are every bit as entitled to respect as men.

But while I agree that women *deserve* respect, I do not believe they *crave* it. Certainly not in the same way most men do.

The thing women crave most is love.

I've been around smart, powerful women my whole life. Usually, they are awash in respect. Their talent, intelligence, and wisdom command it.

They find respect wherever they go. Their employers respect their hard work and dedication; their colleagues respect their insights and integrity; their church and charitable organization leaders respect their contributions of time and resources to the various causes; their children's teachers and coaches respect their involvement and commitment; even their neighbors respect their polite disposition and manicured yards.

Respect is all around them. But love? That is something else entirely. Love is not so easy to find and often even harder to keep.

For a woman to be loved by a man—deeply, passionately, unconditionally, with all that he is towards all that she is—that is a rare thing indeed.

It's an ephemeral thing that cannot be earned the way respect can. But it's a gift a husband can give to his wife every day of her life. And when he does, it is both beautiful and magical.

> "I like not only to be loved, but also to be told I am loved." -
>
> - George Eliot

There are countless ways to demonstrate your love, but women still like to hear it spoken. Open and continuing communication is key.

My father-in-law used to brag (presumably tongue-in-cheek), "I told my wife I love her on our wedding day and promised to let her know if that ever changed." His implication was clear: Once should be enough.

But it isn't.

Not for most women. Not by a long shot.

Chapter 25 – Verbally Express Your Love

Once a day would be a closer approximation, and even that may still fall a little short of how often your wife would like to hear verbal assurances of your love.

Of course, words not backed with action are meaningless: Remember Christ's parable of a father who asked his two sons to come work in the field with him?

The first son said, "Sure. I'll be right there," but never showed up.

The other son initially refused, but later regretted it, sought out his father, and worked alongside him for the rest of the day.

The question Jesus then posed to his listeners is this: Which son actually obeyed? The same principle applies to love as applies to obedience.

> "It takes three seconds to say, 'I love you,' but a lifetime to mean it."
>
> - Justine Jones

If forced to choose between the two, your wife would probably rather have you demonstrate your love for her through your actions without expressing it in so many words than to have you repeatedly declare, "I love you," then behave in a way that contradicts what you've said. Hollow affirmations don't carry a lot of clout.

But why make her choose, when it's within your power to do both? Show her you love her. Yes, by all means. But then speak your love, as well.

Tell her you love her. Tell her how much you love her. Tell her what you love most about her.

Tell her clearly. Tell her sincerely. Tell her often. Then back it all up in the way you treat her.

Put It into Practice:

✍ If you didn't grow up in a home where lots of verbal affirmations of love were spoken, you may feel a little stiff or awkward at first saying, "I love you" in so many words (especially if you haven't uttered those words since your wedding day). Do it anyway. Your wife needs to hear it, and you need to get comfortable saying it—and, with enough practice, you will.

✍ Verbally expressing your love does not preclude using a variety of approaches. You can text it to her. Call her. Write her. Email her. Whisper "I love you." Sing "I love you." Hire a plane to spell "I love you" in the sky. You're limited only by your imagination.

✍ Your wife needs to know that you love her unconditionally—that your love is not contingent on her keeping her figure or cooking great meals or contributing a certain percentage of the family income. So assure her of that fact.

✍ While she hopes your love isn't *based* on external, ever-changing things such as beauty, talent, and success, your wife still likes to know such things are noticed and appreciated. So do your best to strike a balance: "Honey, you know I love you no matter what you wear, but man, do you ever look terrific in that dress tonight!"

Love for
a Lifetime

Afterward

Scripture urges a husband to love his wife and a wife to respect her husband. The Biblical model really does work, regardless of which spouse is the initiator.

In our relationship, my wife is the one who decided to be respectful even when I wasn't being loving. But it didn't take me long to catch on, and our lives have been infinitely better ever since. I like to think of it as the peaceful non-violence of Ghandi or Martin Luther King, Jr. applied to marriage!

As I noted in the introduction, Christ basically gives us two commands—we are to *LOVE GOD* with all our hearts, souls, minds and strength, and we are to *LOVE OTHERS* as we love ourselves.

This book is merely an attempt to give some concrete examples of how that second command to love others can be followed within the context of marriage.

Each chapter details practical suggestions for loving your wife in a sacrificial way and for putting her needs ahead of your own. If you disagree with that premise, then arguing over the details is pointless. Likewise, if you agree with the premise, then the details can be tailored to your own situation.

> "If you want to change a marriage, change the man."
>
> - Justin Buzzard

The real question is whether or not putting others ahead of yourself is a valid approach to life in general or to marriage in particular.

Modern psychological theory claims that the best approach to relationships of all types is "tit-for-tat." A little *"You scratch my back, I'll scratch yours,"* or maybe even *"An eye for an eye, a tooth for a tooth."*

If you always give, such a philosophy posits, then people take advantage of you; if you always take, then people begrudge you. Our goal, they would argue, is to find a happy balance between the two!

Christianity says, *forget about balance.*

Give generously, and don't worry if others take advantage of you. *"If a man asks you to walk with him for one mile,"* Jesus tells us, *"go with him two. If he strikes you on the cheek, turn to him the other also."* (see Matthew 5:39-41)

Christ also calls us to walk in forgiveness: Even if someone sins against us *"seventy times seven,"* we are to forgive them. This is the example Jesus set for us on the cross when he cried out, *"Father, forgive them, for they don't know what they're doing!"* (Luke 23:34, NASB)

So did Stephen, when he was stoned. So did early Christians who were killed in the arenas of Rome. So have countless martyrs down through the ages, even to this very day in Sudan.

That doesn't sound very balanced, does it? It neither protects self nor serves selfish interests. In fact, this response is so unusual and contrary to our instincts that I will go on record as calling it supernatural.

> "We think that forgiveness is weakness, but it absolutely is not; it takes a very strong person to forgive."
>
> - T.D. Jakes

To have that level of love for your fellow man— to be concerned for the welfare of your enemies even as they slay you—requires a strength that none of us possesses on our own.

God alone can give you that kind of power.

And He will, if you ask Him.

Then you can take that supernatural power, strength, and love, and channel it towards your spouse. That's the sort of thing a "to do" list can never really capture.

Plato is said to have taken general principles and derived specifics from them. Aristotle is said to have taken the specifics of life and derived general principles from them.

We hope our books (my *25 Ways to Show Love to Your* Wife and my wife's *25 Ways to Communicate Respect to Your Husband*) will help couples to do a little of both in regards to their marriages. By reading over the specific examples listed, we hope you will be able to see the over-arching theme of putting your spouse's needs ahead of your own and be inspired to *"consider others as more important than yourself."* (Philippians 2:3)

Once you start to view your spouse in that light, you can fill in the details in whatever way makes sense in your specific circumstances.

It is our earnest prayer that God will steel your resolve to be the loving husband He has called you to be, that He will *"thoroughly equip you for every good work"* (2 Timothy 3:17), and that He will lavish His richest blessings upon your life and marriage.

Recommended Reading

The dual goals of being a wise, godly husband and building a strong, happy home are ones every married man should pursue with a lifelong passion and tireless determination.

As much as my wife and I would like to tell you that, once you get past the first fifteen or twenty or twenty-five years of marriage, you'll be able to prop up your feet and coast the rest of the way, such has not been our experience.

Nor have we ever met any older couples who've indicated it's all smooth sailing after forty or fifty or sixty years, either.

25 Ways to Show Love to Your Wife

One thing you can do to invest in your marriage is to read (and implement!) wise counsel from marriage-building resources such as these personal favorites:

Books:
5 Love Languages (Gary Chapman)
If Only He Knew (Gary Smalley)
For Men Only (Shaunti Feldhahn)
Love and Respect (Emerson Eggerichs)
Love for a Lifetime (James Dobson)
Love Your Husband/ Love Yourself (Jennifer Flanders)
Marriage Builder (Larry Crab)

Websites:
All Truth is God's Truth (this one is my blog)—
        http://alltruthisgodstruth.com
Desiring God (John Piper's blog)—
        http://www.desiringgod.org/
Focus on the Family (Jim Daly, president)—
        http://www.focusonthefamily.com/
For the Family (Pat and Ruth Schwenk)—
        http://forthefamily.org/
Loving Life at Home (this one's my wife's)—
        http://lovinglifeathome.com/

Many
Thanks

Acknowledgements

I want to begin by thanking God for giving me the wonderful wife that He has. When we met, I was just a teenager who was infatuated with an extremely smart and very attractive redheaded girl I'd noticed on my college campus. God knew that she was so much more than what I was able to see and that she'd become even more still, and so He graciously orchestrated this "match made in heaven."

I'd also like to thank my lovely and talented wife. I literally cannot imagine a more wonderful partner and spouse. It is a privilege just to know you; being your husband is simply an added bonus that I hardly deserve.

Thank you for being so patient with me over the years. You truly are my better half.

I want to thank all twelve of our children, as well. You are our magnum opus. Each of you is unique and special to us, but you're also just wonderful human beings. We are so happy God has placed you in our family and grateful to see Him at work in your hearts every day.

Thanks to my parents, who have been married for over fifty-two years as of this writing, for setting such a good example of loyalty and faithfulness. The same goes for my in-laws, who had been married for forty-six years before my father-in-law passed away. It is a rarity for couples to actually stay together "until death do us part," but they did, and we are inspired by their commitment. Likewise, my younger sister and my wife's younger sister have each been happily married for over twenty years to our fantastic bothers-in-law. Thank you both for looking after our little sisters!

All together, including our oldest son's eight-year marriage, we have nearly one hundred and eighty years of unbroken marriages across three generations in our family. That is quite a heritage, and one for which we give God all the praise and glory!

Thanks to all our dear friends at church, work, school, and play. So many of you have given wise counsel and a listening ear over the years, and I am grateful. I wish each of you all the happiness and joy in your marriage that we have experienced in ours, minus the hardships and heartaches.

Doug Flanders
January 29, 2015

- Endnotes -

INTRODUCTION: WHERE'S THE LOVE?

1. *"But wishing to justify himself, he said to Jesus, 'And who is my neighbor?'"* (Luke 10:29, NASB)

CHAPTER 1: LISTEN

1. I personally know many wonderful, caring, and compassionate physicians who do their best to listen to patients, despite increasingly heavy workloads. But unfortunately, they've become the exception rather the rule.
2. To view Jason Headley's hilarious YouTube video, "It's Not About the Nail," please follow this link: https://www.youtube.com/watch?v=-4EDhdAHrOg
3. *"Likewise, husbands, live with your wives in an understanding way, showing honor to the woman as the weaker vessel, since they are heirs with you of the grace of life, so that your prayers may not be hindered."* (1 Peter 3:7, NASB)
4. Stephen R. Covey, *The 7 Habits of Highly Effective People: Powerful Lessons in Personal Change*, p. 14.

CHAPTER 2: COMMUNICATE

1. *"But speaking the truth in love, we are to grow up in all aspects into Him who is the head, even Christ."* (Ephesians 4:15, NASB)
2. *"If any of you lacks wisdom, you should ask God, who gives generously to all without finding fault, and it will be given to you."* (James 1:5, NIV)

CHAPTER 4: PRAY FOR/WITH HER

1. Ruhnke, R. *For Better and For Ever,* as quoted by White in *Married To Jesus,* p. 102.

2. *"Again I say to you, that if two of you agree on earth about anything that they may ask, it shall be done for them by My Father who is in heaven."* (Matthew 18:19, NASB)

CHAPTER 6: DON'T LEAVE THE SEAT UP

1. For more information on Van Halen's standard performance contracts and their infamous M&M test, check out this link: http://www.snopes.com/music/artists/vanhalen.asp

CHAPTER 7: THROW DIRTY CLOTHES IN THE HAMPER

1. This may not have been the original intent of the Patriarchal Movement, but I've seen its teachings repeatedly twisted in practice to suggest that women and children should be seen and not heard, and that a wife should never question anything her husband does. Such is not the recipe for a healthy home or happy marriage.
2. 1 Peter 3:7 reads, *"Likewise, husbands, live with your wives in an understanding way, showing honor to the woman as the weaker vessel, since they are heirs with you of the grace of life, so that your prayers may not be hindered."*
3. Mark 10:45 reads, *"For even the Son of Man did not come to be served, but to serve, and to give His life a ransom for many."*

CHAPTER 9: LOSEN THE PURSE STRINGS

1. This story was beautifully recounted by Kim Yeles Meyer and recorded by Chelsea E. Thauwald in an article entitled "Stories from the Heart" and published in a monthly neighborhood magazine called *The Woods Living.* (June 2014, pp. 30-32)
2. Proverbs 15:17 reads, *"Better is a dish of vegetables where love is than a fattened ox served with hatred."*

Endnotes

CHAPTER 10: PRACTICE SERVANT-LEADERSHIP

1. *"Let not many of you become teachers, my brethren, knowing that as such we will incur a stricter judgment."* (James 3:1) King James translates this, *"Be not many masters, knowing that we shall receive the greater condemnation."*
2. "Do nothing from selfishness or empty conceit, but with humility of mind regard one another as more important than yourselves; do not *merely* look out for your own personal interests, but also for the interests of others." (Philippians 2:3-4, NASB)
3. Famous quote from the 2002 Columbia Pictures action adventure movie starring Toby Maguire as Spiderman.

CHAPTER 11: INTIMACY IS A TWO-WAY STREET

1. For a great discussion of the benefits of prioritizing sex in marriage, see my wife's first book, *Love Your Husband/ Love Yourself: Embracing God's Purpose for Passion in Marriage.* (Prescott Publishing, 2010) I cannot count the number of comments I've received from grateful husbands with wives whose attitudes towards sex have been totally transformed after reading it.

CHAPTER 12: GIVE HER TIME TO HERSELF

1. Even Jesus needed time alone, as we see in the following passages:
   - Matthew 14:23—*"After He had sent the crowds away, He went up on the mountain by Himself to pray; and when it was evening, He was there alone."* (Matthew 14:23, NASB)
   - Mark 1:35—*"In the early morning, while it was still dark, Jesus got up, left the house, and went away to a secluded place, and was praying there."*
   - Luke 5:16—*"And He withdrew himself into the wilderness, and prayed."*

25 Ways to Show Love to Your Wife

CHAPTER 15: USE GOOD HYGIENE

1. Kari Friedlander, "9 Celebrity Confessions of Poor Hygiene."
2. Walter Isaacson, *Steve Jobs*, p. 43

CHAPTER 16: LIMIT THE GROSS STUFF

1. See Matthew 12:43-45 (NASB*)—"Now when the unclean spirit goes out of a man, it passes through waterless places seeking rest, and does not find it. Then it says, 'I will return to my house from which I came;' and when it comes, it finds it unoccupied, swept, and put in order. Then it goes and takes along with it seven other spirits more wicked than itself, and they go in and live there; and the last state of that man becomes worse than the first. That is the way it will also be with this evil generation."*

CHAPTER 17: BE PATIENT

1. The complete text of 1 Peter 3:7 reads thus: "*Likewise, husbands, live with your wives in an understanding way, showing honor to the woman as the weaker vessel, since they are heirs with you of the grace of life, so that your prayers may not be hindered.*"

CHAPTER 20: PROVIDE FOR HER NEEDS

1. Kevin Short, "Here is the Income Level at Which Money Won't Make You Any Happier in Each State."

CHAPTER 23: ACTIVELY SEEK YOUR WIFE'S INSIGHTS

1. C.G.N. Mascie-Taylor, "A biological survey of a Cambridge suburb: Assortative marriage for IQ and personality traits."
2. Helena Pycior, *Creative Couples in the Sciences.*
3. Irin Carmon, "The Wives of Great Male Writers, Chapter 5,000."

- References -

Brizendine, Louann. (2006). *The Female Brain*. New York, NY: Morgan Road Books.

Carmon, Irin. (2010). "The Wives of Great Male Writers, Chapter 5,000." *Jezebel*. Accessed: 1/27/15. http://jezebel.com/5477259/the-wives-of-great-male-writers-chapter-5000/.

Covey, Stephen R. (2003). *The 7 Habits of Highly Effective People: Powerful Lessons in Personal Change*. New York, NY: Simon & Schuster (Fireside Books).

Friedlander, Kari. (2012). "9 Celebrity Confessions of Poor Hygiene." *The Huffington Post*. Accessed: 11/15/2014. http://www.huffingtonpost.com/2012/12/12/9-celebrity-confessions-of-poor-hygiene_n_2285828.html

Isaacson, Walter. (2011). *Steve Jobs*. New York, NY: Simon & Schuster.

Mascie-Taylor, C.G. Nicholas and John B. Gibson. (1979). "A biological survey of a Cambridge suburb: Assortative marriage for IQ and personality traits." *Annals of Human Biology, Vol. 6, No. 1, 1-16*. London, England: Informa Healthcare.

Pycior, Helena, Nancy Slack, and Pnina Abir-Am, editors. (1996). *Creative Couples in the Sciences*. New Brunswick, NJ: Rutgers University Press.

Ruhnke, Robert. (1996). *For Better and For Ever*. San Antonio, TX: Marriage Preparation Resources.

Short, Kevin. (2014). "Here is the Income Level at Which Money Won't Make You Any Happier in Each State." *The Huffington Post*. Accesssed: 2/1/2015. http://www.huffingtonpost.com/2014/07/17/map-happiness-benchmark_n_5592194.html

More Marriage-Building Resources
- from Prescott Publishing -

25 Ways to Communicate Respect to Your Husband:
A Handbook for Wives

In this companion book to *25 Ways to Show Love to Your Wife,* Jennifer Flanders tackles the topic of communicating respect to one's husband in a way most men will deeply appreciate. Side effects from implementing the principles she sets forth include a more joyful outlook, better communication skills, and a rekindled desire to love on your man!

How to Encourage Your Husband:
Ideas for Revitalizing Your Marriage

A veritable treasure trove of ideas and suggestions for investing in your marriage and prioritizing your relationship to your spouse, *How to Encourage Your Husband* will benefit couples, whether they've been married 24 hours or 24 years. Get your copy today!

Love Your Husband/ Love Yourself:
Embracing God's Purpose for Passion in Marriage

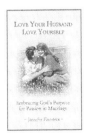

"This book is the talk your mother never had the nerve to have with you." Packed with loads of Biblical wisdom, scientific studies, and humorous anecdotes, *Love Your Husband/ Love Yourself* is a must read for every married woman. It will help you unlock the secret to a happy, healthy, loving, lifelong relationship with your spouse.